THE GHOST T

Acknowledgements

Edinburgh Evening News, The Sun, the *Daily Record, Sunday Telegraph, Dundee Courier, Daily Mirror,* Radio Scotland, Radio 1, Polish National Television, GMTV, BBC 1 *Heaven and Earth Show,* Discovery Channel, History Channel, Learning Channel, Fox Family Channel.

THE GHOST THAT HAUNTED ITSELF

The Story of the McKenzie Poltergeist

Jan-Andrew Henderson

MAINSTREAM
PUBLISHING

EDINBURGH AND LONDON

Thanks to Claire and Sarah for all the invaluable work they did.
Also Katherine, Kate, Cara, Andrew, Duncan, David, Derek, Joy and Gillian.
Each helped in their own unique way.

First published in Great Britain in 2001 by
MAINSTREAM PUBLISHING COMPANY (EDINBURGH) LTD
7 Albany Street
Edinburgh EH1 3UG

ISBN 1 84018 482 5

Reprinted 2003

A catalogue record for this book is available from the British Library

Typeset in Allise and Bembo
Printed and bound in Great Britain by
Cox & Wyman Ltd, Reading, Berkshire

There is a legend that some of the world's most famous fictional monsters and villains were born in Greyfriars churchyard, Edinburgh, Scotland.

In a visit to the cemetery in 1841, Charles Dickens misread the tombstone of a man called Scroggie and invented Ebenezer Scrooge. Robert Louis Stevenson, who wrote *Dr Jekyll and Mr Hyde*, used to sit in the peace and quiet of the graveyard to come up with inspiration for his stories. Polidori, writer of the first vampire story – which heavily influenced the novel *Dracula* – studied just beyond the cemetery wall and Bram Stoker also visited Greyfriars while writing this seminal novel. Mary Shelley was on honeymoon in Edinburgh at the height of the bodysnatching period, when 'resurrection men' dug up bodies from Greyfriars and sold them to scientists for their experiments. Shortly afterwards, she wrote *Frankenstein*.

The story of the Mackenzie Poltergeist, however, is true. When I was asked, or when I felt I should, I changed the names of participants to protect their anonymity. My thanks to all those who came forward and wrote down their accounts. In recreating actual incidents I have allowed myself what I hope is a suitably dramatic turn of phrase – but never at the expense of the facts.

In a country like this
Our ghosts outnumber us
DOUGLAS DUNN (1942–) 'AT FALKLAND PALACE'

If you ask, how do I know I have received God's grace? The answer is: If you
know with certainty that God exists, then you have received it; if not, not.
CHARLES VAN DOREN, *A HISTORY OF KNOWLEDGE*

If only God would give me some clear sign! Like making
a large deposit in my name at a Swiss bank.
WOODY ALLEN (1935–)

Contents

Prologue

What do people need to believe? Now, there's a question that can be taken more than one way. One might say that all we need to believe is the capacity for abstract thought – it often seems we need precious little else. People have believed in fairies, Valhalla and the necessity of the Berlin wall. Sometimes what once seemed obvious to us all turns out to be completely wrong. People believed the world was flat. It was a good guess. Seemed right. It wasn't until science built up enough evidence to the contrary that everyone came to accept the world was round. Yet there are still many who can't really understand why we don't fall off.

In the end, it doesn't matter. We accept the world is round. We don't fall off.

So. What do we *need* to believe?

Do we need to believe that we are not alone? No. There are lonely people. They live. They may not live happily, but they live.

Do we need to believe there is a point to life? Do we need to believe there is something for us after we die?

Again, no, though it is certainly depressing to hold such points of view.

But perhaps we *want* to believe. We want very much to believe that there is something greater than us. Something we don't understand. A point that nobody gets, not even the geniuses. Something that science can't pick apart and make us feel like children. For that we have faith, a belief so strong that it doesn't need evidence. Faith in astrology. Faith in reincarnation. Faith in God.

It is hard to have faith. Scientists tell us we *do* need evidence, that we are fooling ourselves and we have faith in science, so we are dispirited and torn. So we look for evidence of the existence of something, anything, that science and the rational mind are at a loss to explain.

We look for ghosts.

If you say you have been reincarnated you are treated like an idiot; nobody accepts you were really abducted by aliens and only psychopaths believe they have talked to God. But ghosts? So many people claim to have seen one. Can they all be deluded? Perhaps. There are precious few photographs of spectres that don't look as though someone inadvertently put their thumb in front of the camera. It could be that eighteenth-century highwayman you saw outside the window was on his way to a fancy-dress party. It's easy to doubt your own mind in the cold light of day.

A poltergeist is a different matter. Poltergeists move things. They are physical. There may be a scientific explanation for this phenomenon – but that discipline, for all its doggedness, has so far failed to come up with a satisfactory one. Maybe scientists aren't trying hard enough. Perhaps they don't believe enough to really explore the phenomenon. If so, shame on them, for there are few unexplained things left to explore. The defence of the rational mind is that historical poltergeists are the product of ignorance and modern cases are hoaxes. They cite the Amityville or Enfield poltergeists – two of the best-documented cases in history – as proof. Both turned out to be fakes. The witnesses were misrepresented, or had something to gain. 'Evidence' turned out to be manufactured. It's hard to argue with that.

In the two years between 1999 and 2001 there have been over 70 recorded sightings of the entity named the 'Mackenzie Poltergeist'. Witnesses to its attacks ran into the hundreds. They were observers who just happened to be there and they had nothing to gain.

If there is an explanation for the Mackenzie Poltergeist, 'didn't really happen' isn't one of them.

This is its story.

Gill

Statement given by Gill Bruce on 12 April 2001. Gill is a 21-year-old student studying at the University of Edinburgh, Scotland.

I worked over Christmas 2001 in a gift shop and, on my way home after work, I stopped in to see a friend of mine called Ben Scott. His house looks over Greyfriars graveyard, which I have always found fascinating as well as a bit macabre.

Ben had told me about the poltergeist which is supposed to haunt Greyfriars and had commented that the house seemed to have a 'resident ghost'. He thought this was very funny, but I couldn't see how living in a haunted house, in a graveyard, could be a laughing matter.

We were sitting having coffee in his living-room when we heard the toilet flush in the bathroom, just outside the living-room door. 'It likes the bathroom,' Ben said. I know that doesn't sound exactly terrifying, but it sent a chill up my spine. There was nobody else in the house to flush the toilet and no mistaking what the noise was.

I might have brushed it off, but the next time I went to Ben's house there was another 'incident'. Ben was sitting in his living-room with his friend Duncan when I arrived. They told me they had heard what sounded like someone jumping around in the spare room, though there was nobody else in the house. Again, I didn't believe it and thought they were making fun of me – but suddenly there was a tremendous crash from the spare room. There was no mistaking where the sound came from and, of course, we went to see what it was.

The room was completely empty.

The City of the Dead

Cauld blaws the nippin' north wi' angry south
And showers his hailstanes frae the Castle Cleugh
Owr the Greyfriars, whare at mirkest hour
Bogles and spectres wont to take their tour
FROM 'THE GHAISTS: A KIRKYARD EPILOGUE' BY ROBERT FERGUSSON (1750–74)
(DIED AT 24 IN BEDLAM ASYLUM JUST OUTSIDE GREYFRIARS GATES)

Two weeks ago Lisa Allen from Boston visited the
Graveyard on the tour. She said, 'There was no doubt this
was real. I felt it and I never want to feel it again.'

'Is this graveyard the home of Edinburgh's scariest
poltergeist?'
EDINBURGH *Evening News*, 3 JULY 1999

On the day after Christmas, Ben Scott came home from a party
to find blood running down his apartment walls.

This would have been traumatic enough under normal
circumstances, but Ben Scott's circumstances were not exactly
normal. His house was in Greyfriars cemetery – a graveyard that
had long been regarded in Edinburgh lore as home to an
impressive variety of ghosts and spectres. A cemetery that had,
in recent years, become famous as the site of a supernatural
entity known as the 'Mackenzie Poltergeist'. To make matters
worse, Ben Scott's job involved taking nightly tours round the
graveyard to show visitors 'The Covenanters' Prison' – a locked
section of the cemetery. In that section was a tomb nicknamed
'The Black Mausoleum' and this, supposedly, was where the
Mackenzie Poltergeist could be found.

If Ben Scott had been a believer in the paranormal he might

have wondered if the Mackenzie Poltergeist hadn't just paid him a visit in return. But he didn't believe in that kind of thing.

He took off his coat and put it on a coat hook. Then he got a chair, pushed it against the wall, stood on it and looked carefully at the red stains. The substance had dried but it certainly looked like blood. Ben licked his finger, ran it down a discoloured patch of wall and was about to put it to his lips when he thought better of it. He really didn't want to know what this stuff tasted like.

He considered the possibilities. The whole thing could be a practical joke by his friends, though he couldn't begin to imagine them playing a prank this elaborate. Even so, he got off the stool and checked his windows. Outside in the graveyard, tombstones poked granite heads through pristine snow, each ancient marker topped with a frosty halo. Even the trees were crowned with thorns of ice. It was the first white Christmas Ben could remember for years. He looked down. The snow was unbroken below both windows and the windows themselves were still fastened shut.

Ben got a flashlight from his cupboard, fetched a short ladder from the hall and stood it under the small trapdoor in the ceiling. He laboriously hoisted himself through the dark square and toppled into the attic.

'This is a hell of a thing to be doing at Christmas,' he groaned to himself. 'Especially with a hangover.'

He began to crawl gingerly across the cold attic slats, the weak beam of light from his torch wobbling around in the darkness. He had never been up here before, and his eyes made out boxes of forgotten toys from someone else's childhood. The beam of light suddenly gleamed off a pair of beady eyes staring into his own.

'Aaaaaaaaaaaaaaaaaaaaaaaaargh!!! Oh, hello teddy.'

Ben shone the torch behind the tatty stuffed bear and, seeing something else glisten, shuffled closer and ran his fingers over a wooden roof beam. It was wet.

'Aha!' he said softly, a smug grin on his face.

Ben's parents came down from the north that afternoon, bearing gifts. His mother watched as he excitedly tore apart a huge, ribbon-infested parcel.

'It's a garden ornament,' Ben held up a silver-painted plaster cherub. 'That's lovely. No, really, it is.'

'I know you don't have a garden,' said his mother, 'but I thought it would go well with your surroundings.' She nodded furtively towards the graveyard outside, as if the present was designed to appeal to the dead residents as well.

Ben's father stood, hands in pockets, and looked around. 'What's that muck over a' the walls?' Ben had tried to clean off the red stains with a damp cloth, but had only succeeded in spreading them around in wide, rusty swabs. It looked like he had engaged in a ritual slaughter, then unsuccessfully tried to hide the evidence.

'The thermostat on my boiler broke.' Ben pointed to the cupboard where the boiler was kept. 'The water started boiling and forced steam up the overflow pipe and onto the roof. The steam melted the snow, the water ran back down the pipe, hit the top of the boiler, evaporated and spread out across the roof under the wallpaper.'

'Why does your roof hae wallpaper on it anyway?' Ben's father was never one to let a good explanation go uninterrupted.

'It was like that when I moved in. Anyway. Under the wallpaper, the water must have picked up rust or some kind of red dirt. When it reached the walls it started to run down, carrying the red stuff with it.'

'But there's nae join between the wallpaper on the roof and the wallpaper on the wall.' His father peered upwards. 'And how come there's nae red marks on the roof?'

'I don't know,' Ben sighed. 'I'll repaint the walls.'

'You should.' His mother was placing the angel experimentally in different parts of the room. 'It looks like somebody died in here.'

By Christmas 2000, Ben Scott had been taking tours in

Greyfriars churchyard for a year and a half. In that time, he'd seen much to amuse him: he'd witnessed people collapse, apparently 'attacked' by the Mackenzie Poltergeist. He'd lost count of the cuts and bruises visitors claimed had been inflicted on them by something they couldn't see, and had watched with amusement as psychics bumbled among the granite tombs pointing out deceased residents at every turn. He'd smiled when hysterical women on the night walks he led insisted something was touching their hair in the dark.

Ben couldn't believe that people really fell for that kind of stuff. Yes, it was creepy as hell in the graveyard. Once or twice, when he had gone in alone to retrieve a forgotten flashlight, he'd almost had the screaming heebie-jeebies himself – who wouldn't? It wasn't that Ben believed he might see a ghost – he was more scared that some escaped convict might jump out at him from behind a gravestone. Or a serial killer. Or a giant, mutant crab woman from Pluto.

Greyfriars at night had a powerful influence on the imagination.

But the graveyard didn't scare Ben Scott, and neither did its so-called poltergeist. There were plenty of real monsters in the world to do that and just as many demons in the mind.

There was no doubt, of course, that visitors really did collapse in the cemetery; Ben's tours had an average of one a month. Ben could almost swear he himself had heard whispering and rattling noises in the tombs and he had certainly seen the mysterious cuts and bruises that visitors picked up on his walks. He even had photographs of them.

But Ben wasn't easily convinced. It was dark in the cemetery and the tour parties huddled together, as social niceties gave way to an atavistic fear of the unknown. Anybody who had a couple of terrified strangers hanging on to them for dear life was bound to acquire a few bruises. It was the same when people fell over – all it took was an impressionable mind, a bit of abject terror and a touch of claustrophobia.

All right. So 27 collapses in a year and a half did seem a bit excessive – many of the victims hadn't seemed impressionable or frightened, and most of the cuts and bruises had appeared on people who were standing on their own. But if Ben couldn't come up with a logical explanation in every case, it certainly didn't mean that some invisible entity was slapping the paying customers around.

Besides, attacks were great for business – people *wanted* a genuine brush with the supernatural. It was proof that humans were more than eventual worm fodder. So what if it was all in the visitors' minds?

Ben Scott loved the Mackenzie Poltergeist.

A few days later, Ben had a nightmare. He dreamed he climbed through the trapdoor in his ceiling – only this time he came out, not in the attic, but on top of one of the ancient mausoleums that were scattered throughout the cemetery. Greyfriars was spread out in front of him, teeming with worms of moonlight. Ben felt cold and resigned, as if he had sat here, night after night, for many years. The tomb was where his house ought to be, but he realised he could see all the way across the graveyard to the Covenanters' Prison – the church that should have been in the way was no longer there. He knew this was how it often was with dreams; they removed obstacles that couldn't be overcome in the real world.

As he watched, he saw a tall, thin figure with spindly limbs and the body of a concentration camp victim come skipping backwards through the cemetery gates. It was dancing a horrible clown jig, a puppet dance, all arms and legs and wobbling pirouettes. As part of the dance the figure kept leaping backwards into the air – impossibly huge springs – 30 feet, then 25, then 20, landing awkwardly, as if the effort of making each jump were becoming more and more taxing. Each time, it came down closer to Ben Scott's tomb. The figure's long leather coat was in tatters and it jerked around like a big black bird that had been shot in the air. With one last exhausted spring, it landed on the grass directly below Ben, staggering badly now, still facing away. Hopping and panting, it continued the frantic movements, breath whistling from a ragged throat, gathering its strength for another leap.

Though he was terrified of this tapping, whispering monstrosity, Ben couldn't stand the thought that the figure might continue past. More than anything, he did not want to be alone again, to have to climb back into that tomb. In desperation he started to dance as well, trying to move the way the figure was moving, to show he was a kindred spirit. He danced a dance of friendship, hopping up and down and waving his arms around his head. Then he saw the figure's back quiver and thought it was going to jump again and not notice him. So Ben Scott flapped his arms harder, stamping his feet madly on top of the tomb like a lunatic tap-dancer, until the figure whirled round, glaring up at him, its eyes bulging and spittle spraying from its mouth. 'Not danthing!' It screamed at Ben Scott through the lips of a withered corpse, 'Trying to thtay alive!'

And, hopping and skipping and fighting every inch of the way, it jerked and shuffled backwards until it vanished into the Covenanters' Prison.

Ben Scott woke up thrashing wildly. His partner was sitting up in bed, her back pressed against the wall. 'There's something in here,' she hissed in a tearful voice, clutching the duvet in front of her as if it were a shield. 'There's something in the room.' Ben looked wildly around, not even sure if he was awake. 'You were screaming,' she said quietly.

But there was nothing in the room, and next morning both laughed about how ridiculous they must have looked, terrified and holding each other in the dark.

In January, residents of three houses bordering the graveyard began to complain of poltergeist activity in their homes. Being intimately connected with the Mackenzie Poltergeist and living in an identical setting, Ben's thoughts, naturally, turned to this. He began to think about his own place and how strangely the human mind worked. It seemed to Ben that, in the month since Christmas, there had been something odd about his flat – he hadn't considered this until he heard about the other houses. There had been little incidents, nothing he couldn't explain, nothing paranormal, but put them all together and it was just a little . . . disconcerting. His alarm clock, for instance, never seemed to go off at the time he had set it. Annoyed, he asked his partner if she was playing a repetitive practical joke.

'No, Ben. I have a life.'

Ben couldn't recall ever having so many personal things go missing in such a short space of time and none of them ever turned up again. But then, everyone misplaces things – who hasn't found their house keys in the fridge once or twice? At night he would wake to the crash of framed pictures falling off the walls. So what? The plaster must be weak. Ben just wished they would fall off during the day, when the bang wouldn't scare the living daylights out of him. The hands of clocks seemed to loosen or stick; well, they must be cheap, poor quality. Light bulbs blew all the time; cheap wiring. A repulsive smell hung in the air by the living-room door for two weeks; spilled garbage that had finally rotted away.

It was just odd that none of this had ever happened before.

One morning in February, at four a.m., Ben heard screaming right below his bedroom window. He leaped out of bed and looked out but nobody was there. The next day he found a dead gull on the grass, one side a mangled mass of stringy red flesh. At first glance he thought a cat had got it, then he worked out the bird had somehow been mangled by an industrial fan set into the wall below his window. The cover of the fan looked as though it had been pulled off, but he still couldn't see how the bird's wing could have become trapped. Birds were stupid, but not that stupid.

It looked like the gull had been shoved into the blades.

Ben's bathroom door had a bead curtain in front of it. An eyesore, he knew, but he had got it second-hand and it was made of bright green plastic which matched the bathroom's day-glo décor. One night as he lay in bed, he heard the bathroom door swing open, then bang shut, swing open, bang shut. He figured it was due to a draught in the hall, though he'd never felt one there. With each bang the bead curtains would swish and clink, swish and clink. Finally Ben got up and shut the door properly, making certain he clicked the latch, then went back to bed. Just as he was drifting off to sleep, his partner shook his arm. 'The bead curtains,' she said simply. Ben heard them swish again, this time not the gentle movement caused by a draught but the loud jingling they made whenever a person walked through them.

For the next month the curtains clanked regularly, always at night, as if the bathroom were haunted by someone with a weak bladder. Ben gave up trying to work out what was causing it and started trying to ignore it.

In early March Ben called a plumber. Something seemed to be wrong with all the pipes in this house. They had begun to bang and pop and the water would spurt, then stop, spurt then stop. The plumber was a short, cheerful man and, as he sat at the breakfast bar drinking coffee, Ben could hear him whistling as he worked in the bathroom. The sun was streaming through the window, a hazy wash which unfolded fans of light into the large pine-floored room and illuminated motes of dancing dust. Ben made a mental note to give the place a spring clean.

The living-room door opened and the plumber put his head round. 'The strangest thing happened to me yesterday,' he said. Ben presumed that this was how plumbers always began conversations.

'What happened to you yesterday?' he asked, waiting for the punchline.

'I was working on your plumbing,' said the plumber. Nothing unusual so far. 'I heard the bells of Greyfriars ring, then, all of a sudden, I got very cold and sick. I thought I was going to fall over.'

Ben's coffee stopped halfway to his lips. Steam trailed across his vision and vanished into the tide of light. He glanced over his shoulder, through the sunny window to the graveyard outside.

These were exactly the symptoms that visitors described on his tours before they collapsed.

'Then when I woke up this morning I found this.' The plumber rolled up his sleeve and showed Ben his arm.

There was an angry red weal between elbow and wrist.

Ben lay in his bed staring up at the ceiling. It was almost Easter. He had drunk too much and gone to bed alone. As he lay unsuccessfully trying to sleep, he heard a repeated tapping noise just above his head. Ben didn't know what it was, and he no longer cared. A few minutes later he heard the heavy swish of the bead curtains parting. 'I'd take those bloody curtains down if they weren't so classy,' he muttered. Ben was strangely proud of himself for the way he handled these night noises. As a young man he had always had a vivid imagination – couldn't watch horror films. As far back as he could remember, he had always been afraid to spend his nights alone – so he rarely did. Now he found he could lie in bed, close to the lair of the Mackenzie Poltergeist, the entity he shared his life with in so many ways, without being afraid.

Ben Scott couldn't be afraid of the supernatural. He didn't believe in the supernatural. Ben Scott was firmly convinced that he didn't believe in anything.

He tried to drift into sleep, but his mind resisted. For in that drift he lost control of his thoughts and they danced and leapt into places he did not want to go. Hypnogognia, the time between sleeping and waking. The time that turns a person's mind into a soulless tomb, when the horrors in the subconscious crawl up and squat, panting, in their own shadows. The place where a sudden start pulls the sleeper back from staring at the black abyss of his inner self and wakes him in panic.

Ben shot up in bed.

Across the room, something was tapping on the window.

It was a loud tap, a regular tap. The tap of something that wanted attention.

He got out of bed and stumbled towards the window, hands held out in front of him, heart thudding as loudly as the noise he was approaching. The room was black as a tomb. He reached the windowsill, grasped the cord for the blind and pulled. It shot up in a fluid motion and sickly moonlight flooded the room. It was too dark to see far, but the area right below his window was illuminated by a lamp from the graveyard exit. The tapping had stopped the moment he touched the blinds.

There was nobody below his window. There was no place for anyone to hide. There were no tree branches near the glass – there were no trees. Ben opened the window. Lying forlornly on the sill was a small string pouch filled with nuts, which he had bought in the winter hoping to attract birds. It had never worked.

'That's just great,' he growled to whatever feathered intruder was hidden in the shadows. 'This thing sits here for three months and not so much as a bloody nibble. I finally get to sleep and one of you develops a case of the munchies.'

He shut the window and climbed back into bed. Again he lay wanting to sleep but unwilling to succumb, knowing what his half-controlled mind, as it spun slowly into the world of dreams, would tell him.

That the tapping sound was too loud to have been a bird.

That birds don't feed at night.

Megan

Statement taken from Megan Billingsly from Leeds on 17 June 1999. Megan had just left the Covenanters' Prison after being on a walking tour.

My name is Megan. I am 11 years old. When I went into the place first [the Covenanters' Prison], I wasn't frightened. It was very dark and I couldn't see. I was scared then and the man [the tour guide] got me to stand beside him and then I wasn't scared any more. My arms were very cold. When we got outside I went to my mum and took her hand. It was not so dark, but it was still scary. When we got here [Candlemaker Row, the street outside the graveyard] my mum said, what has happened to your arm? There was blood on my arm. I had cuts on it too. My mum said, how did that happen? Is it sore? I didn't know, but it wasn't sore. My arm was very cold and it still feels cold and funny.

Greyfriars

In no part of Edinburgh did summer come up earlier, or with more lavish bloom, than in old Greyfriars kirkyard. Sheltered on the north and east, it was open to the moist breezes of the southwest, and during all the lengthening afternoons the sun lay down its slope and warmed the rear windows of the overlooking tenements.

GREYFRIARS BOBBY, BY ELEANOR ATKINSON

Harder to explain is the Mackenzie Poltergeist, which has generated numerous tales of fire-raising, biting and slapping. The poltergeist has turned up in Greyfriars churchyard.

SCOTLAND ON SUNDAY, SEPTEMBER 1999

Let's take a tour of Greyfriars cemetery. Not a night tour, for at night the graveyard is just a black maw with headstones for teeth. For a place filled with dead people, however, Greyfriars in the daytime is about as pretty a patch of land as you'd care to see. It used to be a garden and still retains a kind of horticultural pleasantness, if you ignore the gravestones. In the fifteenth century the land was still partly rural and belonged to a Franciscan monastery. It wasn't until a century later that Mary Queen of Scots turned the grounds into a burial place to relieve the congestion in St Giles' graveyard.

As the years passed, the city built up around Greyfriars. The emerald lawns, already protected by high medieval walls, became hidden behind rings of massive nineteenth-century tenements as Edinburgh's population exploded. Safe behind this urban barrier, Greyfriars quietly ignored the ravages of the industrial revolution. Today it is probably even more attractive than during the Victorian era, now that many of the uglier surrounding buildings have been demolished. Tenements on the east side of the graveyard still survive, but the massive influx of bodies over the centuries means that the rising sod has partly obscured their walls. On the street side they look out over a narrow road called Candlemaker Row and are five stories high. On the graveyard side, however, only two stories are above ground and there are ornate tombs built against their sides.

By the time the graveyard reaches the north-eastern end, its camber has become even more bizarre. Candlemaker Row runs down into the Grassmarket – one of the city's favourite drinking haunts – and here the graveyard wall rises a good 30 feet above the street. On the other side, however, the bodies come within a foot of the top. Here one can see the Martyr's Monument, a reminder of the hundreds of Covenanter rebels executed in the Grassmarket below and buried inside this earthen strip. Here, a flight of steps leads down to a giant gate separating the graveyard from the revellers across the way. This is one of only two entrances to Greyfriars and, in less 'civilised' times, it was where the heads of executed criminals were displayed on poles as a graphic comment on the wages of sin.

The other gate is at the southern corner where the ground is highest, set back between Greyfriars Bobby's Bar and a row of small shops. Stretching away from this unobtrusive entrance, the western tombs are sheltered by another row of tenements – most of which, like their eastern counterparts, have been converted into offices. Despite its beauty, only a handful of homes are actually within sight of this final resting place. One of those, of course, was the flat which belonged to Ben Scott.

The north-west section of the graveyard is truly breathtaking. From the top of a mountain of sparsely covered bodies, the casual picnicker has an unimpeded view of the splendour of Edinburgh Castle, George Heriot's school and the spires and medieval skyscrapers of the Royal Mile.

Greyfriars cemetery is both sombre and beautiful. In summer the grass becomes lush and verdant and the trees, though old, are strong and healthy – after all, the horticulture here is well fed. Among the greenery, the headstones do not look out of place as they point their rocky fingers towards heaven. The markers are not regulated or uniform like those in a modern cemetery, for nobody has been buried in Greyfriars for almost a century. Instead, each stone is hand carved and individual, with a character all of its own, and this seems appropriate, for surely those they commemorate wanted to be as just unique as when they were alive. Some tombstones lean left, some right. Greyfriars is more like a sculpture than a normal cemetery.

Greyfriars is almost a work of art.

Around the sides of the cemetery the vaults are large and ornate, some three or four times the height of those they commemorate. Each is adorned with skulls, crossbones and angels heralding the day of judgement, carvings that aren't exactly subtle in making their point. 'Your life will end some day,' they say, 'so be careful how you live that life.' Yet these proud and lovingly wrought monstrosities now seem to droop more than the trees. The substance used to make them was sandstone, a material ill suited to prepare delicate carvings to stand up to the ravages of time and weather. Now angels have no noses and demons wear blank expressions rather than demonic ones – and they are all the creepier for it. Even sadder, the writing has faded and left the inhabitants of these great edifices robbed of the one thing they intended to celebrate – their identities.

The kirk itself has weathered well, despite several mishaps. An odd, flat-fronted 'Dutch barn', it was built in 1620, wrecked by Cromwell's roundheads in 1650, accidentally blown up by gunpowder stored there in 1718 and then reconstructed that same year.

As befits a historic graveyard, there are several minor celebrities buried under the gently rolling slopes. Here lie 37 chief magistrates of the city, 23 principals and professors of the university, 33 of the most distinguished lawyers of their day, six Lords President of the Supreme Court of Scotland and 22 senators of the College of Justice. Greyfriars is also the last resting place of George Smellie the printer, James Hogg the poet, William Adam the architect and Captain John Porteous of the city guard, hanged by an unruly mob in 1736; all interesting characters, though their fame, like most of their tombs, has eroded over the years.

There are others below the soil that deserve more recognition than they receive. James Hutton, the 'Father of Modern Geology', has only a tiny plaque on the cemetery wall. You'd expect more for the man who correctly theorised how the earth was formed, then went on to provide proof of its rotation. In an unmarked grave lie the mortal remains of William McGonagall, without doubt the worst poet who ever lived.

> Beautiful City of Edinburgh, most wonderful to be seen,
> With your ancient palace of Holyrood and Queen's Park
>   Green,
> And your big, magnificent, elegant New College
> Where people from all nations can be taught knowledge . . .

Talent like that deserves to be trumpeted from the rooftops but, unfortunately, all McGonagall has is another little plaque with his picture on it. And it's squint.

Even more worthy of fame is James Burnett. A hundred years before Charles Darwin, this Edinburgh advocate wrote a book called *Of the Origin and Progress of Language*, which contained a theory of evolution. Ahead of its time by a century, the idea was ridiculed and stories of Burnett's eccentric notions were told in the city long after he was laid to rest in Greyfriars. Less than a hundred yards away is Edinburgh University Medical Department, where the young Charles Darwin studied for two years. No prizes for guessing in which fertile soil the germ of his famous theory first took root.

Of course, the most famous inhabitant of Greyfriars graveyard is not human at all. It is Greyfriars Bobby, the eponymous dog immortalised in Eleanor Atkinson's book and Walt Disney's movie. Bobby was a Skye terrier owned by a shepherd named John Gray. His master died while Bobby was still a puppy and the little dog spent the next 16 years sleeping on the grave. If this version of the story is true, then the dog was out of luck, for John Gray the shepherd is actually buried in East Preston Street, over a mile away. It doesn't matter in the end – people prefer legends to facts. On Candlemaker Row there sits an effigy of the devoted but directionally challenged pooch, the most photographed statue in Scotland.

There is one last tomb in Greyfriars that should be mentioned. It is an ugly, black vault with a high ribbed dome, topped by something that looks suspiciously like a large Brazil nut. This is the tomb of George Mackenzie, advocate to King Charles II. A major political presence in seventeenth-century Scotland, his fame has dwindled over the last three centuries. But the name of George Mackenzie has recently become famous once more, for a very different reason.

A few yards from his tomb, in the south-western corner of the graveyard, is a locked gate. Beyond it lies a long, narrow strip of cemetery, bordered by high, vault-studded walls. This is the notorious Covenanters' Prison, once a primitive concentration camp for religious dissenters – and the haunt of the Mackenzie Poltergeist.

Siobhan

Siobhan Reuse from Minnesota, USA, entered the Covenanters' Prison on 20 August 1999. At the time she was a 21-year-old student and was visiting Scotland to see the Edinburgh Arts Festival.

> I had been to all sorts of shows at the festival and thought I would try something different, something Scottish, especially since all the performers I'd seen so far seemed to come from other countries. I picked a walking tour to go on, a ghost tour, not for any particular reason – it was just the first thing I saw that I figured would tell me something about the city. I didn't know what to expect, but it was enjoyable and I found out a lot about Scottish history. The graveyard was a big surprise to me because it must have been 11 o'clock at night and the sky was yellow rather than black. It wasn't even dark! The graveyard looked pretty and not very scary, though with the yellow light it looked very weird. Needless to say, I wasn't scared at all, even though I had come on the tour on my own.
>
> The tour ended inside a tomb called the Black Mausoleum. The tour guide began to tell us of all the creepy things that had happened in this place since the tours began. I felt a bit let down. I was enjoying myself but I knew nothing was going to happen and if he was telling the truth, that was the point of being in this tomb anyway, wasn't it?
>
> Then I just stopped breathing. I can't put it any better than that. I must stress that I wasn't scared or tired or feeling unwell, it was more like something had

put a hand over my mouth and stopped the air getting in. I took two or three steps back and hit the wall then pushed forwards again, trying to get the guide's attention or get out of the tomb. I was absolutely terrified and I remember perfectly the sick feeling in my chest that comes with being so scared. I honestly thought I was going to die.

The next thing I remember was when I woke up outside. I was told I had only been unconscious for a few seconds. The guide gave me his address after the tour and asked if I would write to him and say what had happened. I had decided not to because I felt stupid about the whole thing and there was probably a logical explanation for the way I felt. Then I decided I would write something after all, because I can't deny that it did happen and I have no rational explanation for it.

I will admit that I have never felt anything like that in my life before.

Into The Mouth Of Madness

Behind the Church is the haunted Mausoleum of Sir George Mackenzie: Bloody Mackenzie, Lord Advocate in the Covenanting troubles and author of some pleasing sentiments on toleration.

ROBERT LOUIS STEVENSON, *EDINBURGH PICTURESQUE NOTES* 1890

It has been widely felt that the ghost of George 'Bloody' Mackenzie, the persecutor of the Covenanters, has haunted the site since his death in 1691. The fact that Bloody Mackenzie's body is interned in the same site as those he condemned to death has been mooted as a source of cosmic conflict — potentially meaning that the spirits of both parties are unable to rest.

CLAIRE KNEESHAW, *ABOUT EDINBURGH*, MARCH 2000

December 1998. It was raining hard in Edinburgh and had been for most of the night. The streets of the Old Town shone like black marble and, in Greyfriars churchyard, stray cats sheltered under the flat-topped tombs, the glittering pinpoints of their eyes almost hidden by the cascade. Outside the cemetery, cars roared through dark thoroughfares, sloshing walls of water onto the pavement and eliciting squeals from hardy drinkers dashing, coats over their heads, from one pub to another. Inside Greyfriars the rain was a continual sinister hiss, as if the paths winding between the graves and around the kirk were angry dark snakes.

At around 11 p.m. a hunched, wet figure entered the cemetery. His hair was matted and stuck to his face; his clothes were worn and thick with grime, which was soaking into the fabric under the torrent of water. Normally it wasn't possible to get into Greyfriars at night, since both of the great gates were locked and the wall was too high to climb. But a television crew, filming a BBC drama, had knocked the east gates off by inadvertently backing a truck into them and they had never been replaced. In many ways the gates were not necessary as a deterrent, for few people were desperate to get into Greyfriars after dark. But to this particular homeless man, the cemetery at night wasn't as distressing as the idea of sleeping outside in this downpour. There was a homeless shelter down the street, but some people still spent their nights outside – for reasons that were their own – and at least the cemetery provided peace and some rude shelter. Many of the more ornate tombs had roofs and though they were damp and open to the elements, they were better than a park bench in this kind of weather.

The man took the south-western route round the cemetery, where the ground was highest, heading for the Covenanters' Prison. In 1998 it was still open to the public and the roofs and entrances of one or two tombs there were not yet padlocked shut. To the left of the prison doorway was the tomb of the famous architect James Adams and his family, a fairly enclosed place to shelter, as was the vault next to it.

The homeless man glanced longingly at the tomb of George Mackenzie as he passed it. Now *there* would be a great place to get a semi-decent sleep. Instead of just an iron gate, Mackenzie's tomb had stout wooden doors keeping the chill winter winds at bay. The only opening that could let the elements in was a small barred aperture in the middle of one door. The man walked up the three stone steps to the tomb entrance and peered at the metal clasp holding the doors closed. No luck – there was a padlock fastened through it, and had been as long as he could remember. Still. No harm in looking. One day maybe, it would be different. One day everything might be different.

The homeless man peered into the pitch-black interior of the vault. He pulled a plastic lighter kept dry by several layers of clothing from deep in his pocket, held it through the bars of the window and flicked a flame to life. By its light he could just make out the bottom of the empty stone sarcophagus and it looked dry.

The homeless man sighed. Too bad about the padlock. The tomb would have been the perfect place to shelter, safe from the weather and away from the prying eyes of anyone who might want to disturb him.

Then, for some reason, on this rainy December evening he did something he had never done before. Instead of continuing on to the south-western mausoleums, the man looked around and climbed awkwardly over the railings that ran from the walls of Mackenzie's tomb to the vaults on either side. He landed on wet gravel and felt his way round the back. He had seen something when looking thorough the vault door – a glimmer of light, perhaps – he wasn't sure exactly what. But he decided to find out.

And there it was. Right at the back, where Mackenzie's tomb and the graveyard wall almost met, he felt a small rectangular hole in the wall. He had no idea what the opening was for, maybe ventilation, though why a graveyard vault would need ventilation was anyone's guess. Perhaps it was to let rainwater run out of the tomb. It could be a cat-flap for all the drenched man cared – what mattered was that it was just big enough for him to crawl through.

Seconds later, he was standing inside George Mackenzie's mausoleum. The tomb was cylindrical with a blank stone floor, a floor that was cold and hard but not wet. Not exactly the Hilton, but it was better than a pile of newspapers in some doorway. When his eyes had become used to the blackness, the man noticed that there was a rusted iron grille about the length of a door set into the floor. Flicking his lighter, he brought the bars of the grille into relief and saw that underneath, a flight of steps descended into blackness. He leaned down and gave a tug. The grille gave a little and the man could see that it was hinged.

He had a choice. He could climb back into the rain, find some covering, bring it back and settle down for the night on the floor of George's tomb. Or he could venture down the dark stairway and see if there was anything useful there. Maybe it was even a little warmer at that lower level – after all, it was below ground, and so a natural shelter. Many people would rather freeze than venture down into a pitch-black tomb armed only with a lighter, though it never seems to stop victims in teenage horror movies. But then, most people wouldn't have had the nerve to be standing inside a haunted tomb at night in the first place.

The homeless man gave a mighty tug and the grille rattled up in a shower of rust. Holding the lighter in front of him, he advanced carefully down the stairs. An incredible sight awaited him. The stairs led down to another room, and its function was immediately obvious. In a line were four coffins – one, presumably, the final resting place of George Mackenzie himself. They were huge affairs, ornate and solid as any tomb, but they had stood the test of time better than the edifices dotted round the graveyard above. George had been lying there since 1691 and his coffin, safe from the weather in this dark hole, looked as sturdy as it had when they laid him in it.

People have many motivations. Their wants and fears work by a complicated set of weights and measures which are easily unbalanced: gain weighed against fear, desires versus cultural mores. But circumstance, unnoticed, usually tips the balance and its downwards slope is so gradual that nobody notices the effect. Here was a coffin belonging to someone who had obviously been a rich and powerful gentleman. There might be an expensive brooch inside, or a silver snuffbox, perhaps even a shroud which could be used as a blanket. To break into a coffin that had remained undisturbed for 300 years for such a dubious reward would be a damnable act to most people. We generally tend to shun away from grave-robbing for any reason. Then again, most people don't end up wet and cold and trying to sleep in a graveyard tomb, and it probably seemed to the homeless man that social niceties were the least of his worries.

The balance tipped. He looked around, lifted a stout bit of

wood from the corner of the tomb and began to pound away at the coffin seal. He didn't bother to keep his assault quiet. Who on earth was going to be in a rainy graveyard at this time of night?

Up in the cemetery the dog walker was startled by the sudden noise. It sounded like . . . hammering. He looked around, seeing nothing moving but his dog, sniffing suspiciously round Greyfriars Bobby's grave.

Yet there it was again. A thumping sound, like the graveyard suddenly had a heart – and his own heart began to pound in macabre harmony. It sounded as though something below the sod was getting ready to rise out of a grave and pull him by his turn-ups into the fiery depths of hell.

Greyfriars at night has a certain way of preying on the subconscious.

He felt a tug at his trouser-leg and his heart almost leapt into his head. The dog looked up balefully from his feet, its mouth full of material. 'Good dog,' he whispered. 'Never do that again. Never.' The thumping noise began once more and the dog gave a snuffling start. Its owner looked in the direction of the noise, which seemed to be coming from George Mackenzie's tomb. 'We'd better take a look and see what that is. Stay close to me, dog. Try to look fierce.'

He switched on the flashlight he always carried for these nocturnal jaunts and made his way towards the sound. The dog walker wasn't too keen on investigating this anomaly and neither, for that matter, was his dog. Like many locals he knew that George Mackenzie's tomb had a reputation for being haunted, but there had never been any actual noise from it before.

As if on cue, the hammering noise suddenly stopped. Creeping closer, the man shone his flashlight at the door. The padlock was still in place, still locked.

'I dinnae ken what could be making that noise, but it's bloody creepy,' he said to the dog. 'That'll be why you're sitting away over there and not here protecting me.'

Suddenly there was a crash from inside.

'What the . . .'

Another balance tipped. The dog walker could have run, but he was a practical man and reluctant to believe that some bogey-man was interrupting his nightly constitutional. He crept up the small stone steps and shone his torch through the aperture of Mackenzie's tomb door. Like the homeless man he was a brave soul, which was more than can be said for the dog, which sat panting several yards away, pretending to be interested in a stick.

Down below, the homeless man lay stunned. Hammering away at George's tomb, he had stepped back to get a better swing and toppled backwards through an unseen hole in the floor. Though he hadn't fallen far, it was enough to knock the wind out of him. Dust caught in his throat and beneath his back he felt what seemed to be splintered wood. There must have been planks or some similar covering over a hidden opening, rotted by who knew how many years of existence, ready to give way the moment someone stood on them. The homeless man fished his lighter from his back pocket and flicked it again.

In the quivering flame he saw that what he had fallen into was a long rectangular aperture, more like a shallow cellar than another room. He must have rolled inside, carried by the momentum of his fall, for the roof was only a couple of feet from his upturned face. He turned his head to the side and brought the lighter up to his shoulder.

There was an eyeless head next to his.

With a gasp he jerked away and as he did so, he felt his cheek scrape against something rough. Swallowing, he brought the lighter round. It couldn't be. It couldn't be what it felt like. Another pair of sightless eyes stared into his own. Below them, thick with green mould, rotted teeth grinned a corpse's grin inches from his own trembling lips, as if it wanted to give him a deathly smooch. The homeless man gave a sob and held his lighter out at arm's length. The cellar might once have been much larger but now the ceiling and floor were only feet apart. The whole room looked as if it had been filled with lumpy earth, but this was not ordinary soil. Skulls littered the floor. Skeletal hands pointed accusingly out of their earthy prison. Shinbones and femurs were interlocked and pelvic bones and ribcages fused into each other at grotesque angles, warped by the forces of time, water and soil. A thick fur of green mould covered the whole skeletal landscape. The homeless man was surrounded by an orgy of death – a carpet of dismembered remains. He knew with a horrible certainty that the room was filled not with earth but with earth-covered bodies.

His nerve broke. With a shuddering cry, he scrambled across the corpses, hearing ribs snap and collarbones break, and hauled himself out of the hole, not even noticing the pain as his own shins scraped over the ragged exit and his head banged against the rough stone. As he ran up the stairs and burst out of the grille he began to scream.

The dog walker was nervously shining his flashlight into the empty tomb when the homeless man surged out of the open grille on the floor, turned and stared into the light, eyes rolling and jaw hanging slackly in terror. After a few nights sleeping rough he hadn't looked too pretty to begin with, but now his sodden clothes were matted with green, mouldy soil and his forehead was clotted with blood. Perhaps believing the light was that mythical luminescence you see as you are about to die, he turned and shambled towards it. The dog walker gave a squeak and fell backwards down the stairs.

Seeing the light suddenly extinguished, the homeless man came to his senses and decided that his wisest move was to get out of the tomb, the graveyard and quite possibly the whole city, as quickly as possible. He squeezed himself through the gap at the back of Mackenzie's mausoleum, vaulted over the railing and landed on the graveyard path, right in front of the terrified dog walker who, on his hands and knees, had just found the flashlight he dropped when he had seen the zombie leap through the floor of Mackenzie's tomb.

The dog walker pointed the torch at the apparition looming over him. Shining a torch under a person's chin is always a good way to make them look ghoulish and since this particular person had just emerged, covered in slime, earth and blood from a locked vault, the effect was positively electric. The dog gave a yelp and shot off down the hill towards the graveyard gate. With a remarkably similar noise and at almost the same velocity, its owner followed. The homeless man looked around, trying to see what had terrified them so much. Was something following him out of the vault? He turned and ran after the terrified pair, whose speed increased exponentially, and all three vanished out of the graveyard and down the rainy street.

The police, of course, investigated the incident. They had the tomb unlocked, lifted the grille and walked down the stairs. There they checked Mackenzie's coffin, but it seemed none the worse for wear. Then they peered into the hole. Skeletal hands beckoned and empty sockets glared from the macabre boneyard below. The police couldn't tell how many bodies were there – on the surface there seemed to be about a dozen, but the soil bulged ominously and it looked as if there were many more just below the topsoil. It was a room filled with bodies all right, and nobody in the church seemed to know whose they were or how they got there. It was known that George was not the only person interred in the mausoleum and that, once or twice, people of wealth who admired him had asked to be placed in the tomb. (In 1814, for instance, the widow of Lieutenant Roderick Mackenzie of Linessie was laid there after claiming that Mackenzie was 'nearly related' to her on her mother's side.)

But there were enough people buried at the bottom of Mackenzie's tomb to stage a biblical epic. Were they the corpses of long-dead paupers who had not had enough money to pay for a proper burial? Were they dumped there after the graveyard became too full of corpses to bury anyone new. Had they dug up and thrown into Mackenzie's tomb to make room when overcrowding in the cemetery had reached its peak?

One thing was certain. They had lain down there undisturbed for a long, long time. Feeling they had now been disturbed quite enough in one night to make up for that, the police shut the grille, padlocked the gate and went back to concentrating on more recent crimes.

The first sighting of the Mackenzie Poltergeist took place a week later.

Tony, James, Heather, Allan

Statements taken by members of a tour party who entered the Covenanters' Prison on 15 August 1999. The group retired to the pub afterwards and wrote down what had happened to them.

TONY WILLIAMSON, 31, FROM IOWA:

We were standing inside the Black Mausoleum. It was dark in there but the sky outside was not and it wasn't cold. In fact, it was warmer inside the Black Mausoleum than it was outside because we were now sheltered from the wind. The tour guide [Ben] was very lively telling the stories and I don't think he noticed anything was wrong to begin with. But I had suddenly gotten very cold. And I mean cold. There were big puffs of condensation coming from my mouth. I suddenly felt ill and I wanted very much to get out of the tomb. I am from Iowa, and I don't scare easy, but I felt like I would if I was hunting and realised there was a dangerous animal somewhere near. The others say they heard thumping, but I did not. I went to the pub and wrote this down quickly so I would not forget.

JAMES MARKHAM, 28, FROM WORCESTER:

We were standing inside the tomb and suddenly the air was very, very cold. You could tell the difference from just seconds before. I was at the back and I heard what seemed to be a knocking noise. I looked behind the tomb to see if there was anyone hiding there when I came out but the back of the tomb is up against a wall.

HEATHER STRASSMAN, 22, FROM AUSTRALIA:

I was very scared, but just because we were in a graveyard. I didn't really expect anything to happen. Then the air got very cold and something banged into the back of the wall two or three times. The guide even commented on how cold it had become but he kept talking. I wanted to get out and I looked around and could see other people looking the same way. I was shaking now I was so cold and asked if we could leave. The guide, Ben, wanted to stay and finish his story but I felt like I had to get out. I just could not stay there. Other people around me started to ask to get out too and Ben said, 'All right, then, let's go.'

ALLAN MANN, 23, FROM AUSTRALIA:

I was just wearing shorts because it was a warm night. In the Black Mausoleum I was fine at first, then suddenly I was very cold. One second I was okay, the next I also felt sick. Everybody started asking to leave at the same time and I did not want to go because I wanted to see what would happen but I felt so bad that I had to go too. The guide said 'all right then' and took us out.

It was totally and absolutely weird.

Something Wicked This Way Comes

> In this city of the dead have been interred so vast a
> number of men of eminence that the mere enumeration of
> their names would make a volume . . . Here too lie, in
> unrecorded thousands, citizens of more humble position,
> dust piled over dust, till the soil of the burial-place is now
> high above the level of the adjacent Candlemaker Row
> the dust of those who lived and breathed, and walked our
> streets in days gone by.
>
> *OLD AND NEW EDINBURGH (1880-1883)* BY JAMES GRANT

> I'm looking for some kind of premises. A warehouse, a shop
> . . . anything. But it has to be genuinely haunted . . . and
> it has to be large enough to take people in . . . I might
> make it part of a tour.
>
> BEN SCOTT INTERVIEWED ON *SCOTTISH CONNECTION*, RADIO SCOTLAND, MARCH 1999

In Greyfriars graveyard in 1999, the Mackenzie Poltergeist first
made its presence felt. This was done in an almost leisurely way,
in the manner of something struggling to come fully to life –
or, perhaps, fighting to stay asleep. After all, Greyfriars had
plenty of violence, desecration and misery in its history.

Then again, they say misery loves company.

Death is the ultimate unknown and, for many, the ultimate
fear. The graveyard is the constant reminder of that fact, a focus
for those terrible emotions. And of all the graveyards in all the
cities in all the world, as Humphrey Bogart might have said if
he weren't dead, Greyfriars ranks high as a barometer of human
transience.

Here are just a few instances. During the great plague of
1568, thousands of diseased corpses were flung into a huge pit

in Greyfriars. In 1581 James Douglas, Regent of Scotland, was guillotined outside the north gate for the murder of the Mary Queen of Scots' husband and his headless body was buried in the section of the churchyard reserved for common criminals. The scholar and historian George Buchanan was buried there with great pomp and ceremony in 1582 – then his headstone gradually sank into the earth and vanished. Greyfriars holds the famous anatomists Alexander Monro *primus* and his son Alexander Monro *secundus*, buried in 1767 and 1817 respectively and it was these men and their fellow scientists that brought about yet another of the graveyard's black periods.

From the mid-eighteenth century to the mid-nineteenth century, Edinburgh enjoyed the title 'The Athens of the North' as the centre of the great Scottish Enlightenment. The city led the West in philosophy, architecture, civil engineering, economics, law and science. Edinburgh University was one of the finest in the world – its anatomy department was particularly renowned for its pioneering work in the field of medicine. But to teach it properly, a constant supply of recently deceased bodies was needed, far more than was allotted to anxious medical students and their ambitious professors. Following the newly formed principles of capitalism – formulated by Scots economist Adam Smith – a brisk trade in bodysnatching sprang up to meet the sudden demand for fresh cadavers. Having no watchtower to protect its bodies, and being surrounded by criminal-infested slums, Greyfriars was the favourite location of these 'Resurrection Men'. At night, they would climb over the north wall, where the trees were thickest, and silently make their way to a recently filled plot. There they would scrape away the earth with wooden spades specially designed to prevent the clash of steel on stone, digging straight down at the end where the head of the coffin lay. When the rough wood came into view, they would prise open one end and carefully slide the body out using hooks and ropes – an anatomist would pay less if the corpse showed signs of abuse. The body went into a cloth sack, the vertical hole was filled in again, the soil was patted down – and nobody but the resurrection men and their medical masters were any the wiser.

Greyfriars, like other cemeteries, employed occasional night watchmen, but guards were easily bribed and it was not unusual to see families, rich and poor, huddled round the graves of recently deceased relatives waiting for their loved ones to decompose enough to be useless to the anatomists. In the churchyard today you can still see 'mortislocks', cage-like devices intended to protect newly buried corpses from these entrepreneurs of death.

In one legendary incident, bodysnatchers in Greyfriars pulled an old woman from her resting place and found, to their delight, that she had rings on her fingers. They were happily hacking off the bejewelled digits when she sat up and gave a lusty yell, prompting the grave robbers to depart and, probably, take up a new career. For another of Greyfriars' many idiosyncrasies was that people were sometimes buried alive. In eighteenth-century Edinburgh you didn't need a death certificate to be buried, you simply had to look deceased. In the disease-infested slums of the Old Town, citizens were buried as fast as possible and sometimes before it was properly confirmed that they were actually dead. One Victorian estimate stated that 2 per cent of the population were buried alive and scare stories like this prompted some forward-looking citizens to install little bells in their coffins – a case of wishful thinking if ever there was one. This gruesome estimate was, of course, greatly exaggerated, as befitted a society obsessed with morbid fancy, but excavators have found coffin lids with claw and bite marks on their undersides.

In December 1879, the city authorities gathered together a mass of human skeletons that had been excavated from St Giles' graveyard and from under its adjoining High Kirk. Several tons of bones including, quite possibly, the Covenanting leader, James Graham of Montrose, and the 'Father of Presbyterianism', John Knox, were dumped in Greyfriars without even a marker to show where they ended up.

It was common practice in Greyfriars to bury the dead without headstones. Immense overcrowding, horrific living conditions and daily violence guaranteed the cemetery a continual torrent of bodies. Give them all tombstones and within a short space of time nobody would have been able to see the grass. Instead, only the famous or wealthy were allowed to indicate their last resting place. Gradually the pleasant garden valley levelled out as more and more earth was drafted in to cover over the steadily rising mass of human remains. In time, the valley was transformed into a thinly covered corpse mountain, giving the graveyard the unique shape it holds today.

The situation was impossible to alleviate. By the late-eighteenth century, the Old Town of Edinburgh was crammed to bursting point with the deprived and neglected. The Highland Clearances, the Industrial and Agricultural Revolutions and the Irish potato famine caused a mass immigration of the poor into the city and between the years 1800 and 1830, the population of Edinburgh doubled. In the north of the city, the New Town had sprung up and anyone with enough money moved there. But in the cramped, stinking closes and wynds of the Old Town, the population still suffered unbelievable hardships.

Greyfriars was squarely in the middle of this slum-ridden pool of misery. Against the south wall was the poorhouse. On the west side stood a crude hospital and the Heriot school for orphaned children. Outside the east gate was Bedlam asylum, while the north looked through the Grassmarket gallows to the West Bow, the site where notorious serial killers Burke and Hare hunted and killed their prey.

When the Edinburgh poor died they had not far to go. Most couldn't afford a proper burial – or a coffin for that matter – and were buried as rudely as they had died. The chronicler Arnot, writing in 1779, gave this vivid and depressing description of the cemetery.

> The graves are so crowded on each other that the sextons frequently cannot avoid in opening a ripe grave encroaching on one not fit to be touched. The whole presents a scene equally nauseous and unwholesome. How soon this spot will be so

surcharged with animal juices and oils, that, becoming one mass of corruption, its noxious steams will burst forth with the prey of a pestilence, we shall not pretend to determine; but we will venture to say, the effects of this burying-ground would ere now have been severely felt, were it not that, besides the coldness of the climate, they have been checked by the acidity of the coal smoke and the height of the winds, which in the neighbourhood of Edinburgh blow with extraordinary violence.

Now, that's just not nice at all.

Yet despite this horrifically eloquent warning, the stuffing of bodies into Greyfriars' already packed soil went on for almost another century. Today there are only a few hundred headstones in the graveyard. The number of corpses in this dead metropolis, with no sign to mark their brief existence, are hundreds of times that many.

Ben Scott sat on top of the mountain of bodies, near the east gate, eating a cheese pasty. Filtering through the branches, a weak winter sun cast nets of cold light across a smattering of headstones and, every now and then, Ben inched along the grass to keep ahead of the great crawling shadow of Greyfriars church.

He heard footsteps behind him and turned to see a tall, broad man with cropped sandy hair standing behind him.

'Well, hello there Alaisdair.'

'Ben. How's tricks?'

Alaisdair Watson crouched down next to him and they both admired the view. The two men did not know each other well, but Edinburgh, despite being the capital of the country, has that small-town ambience whereby half the citizens seem to be on nodding terms with the other half. Ben took bus tours round the Highlands, cycle tours round the city and walking tours of the Old Town. He was a familiar sight to many people. Ben wasn't sure exactly what Alaisdair did — all sorts of things as far as he could see – but one of them seemed to be working in the church at Greyfriars.

The two men exchanged pleasantries, in the manner of people who like each other's company but don't really know what to talk about.

Then Alaisdair Watson said something that tipped a balance.

'I heard you on the radio talking about ghost tours.' He tapped the ground in front of him. 'You should do a ghost tour in here.'

Ben looked across the smooth incline, taking in the glimmering spires of the city and the castle with its tiny white Saltire billowing silently in the distance.

'It isn't very scary.'

'Oh. You don't think so?'

Alaisdair smiled and sat down.

'Let me tell you a wee story.' He turned and indicated George Mackenzie's tomb, squatting behind them like a big stone toad. 'Couple of months ago, it was raining hard, quite late at night. Anyway, this homeless guy came into the graveyard looking for somewhere to sleep . . .'

The Mackenzie Poltergeist came to life slowly. Its first breaths were light and hardly felt, merely a hint of what was to come. Visitors to the graveyard began to comment on a strange smell coming from George Mackenzie's tomb and point out that the air around the door seemed unnaturally cold. There was nothing particularly alarming or even unusual about this. Perhaps some animal had become trapped inside and died. And the winter sun crossed the sky behind the offending tomb, so of course it would be cold at the front.

Then, early in 1999, a woman peering into the aperture in the door of Mackenzie's mausoleum staggered backwards down the steps and landed awkwardly on the ground. It was a sight greeted by consternation or amusement by various onlookers, depending on what type of person they were. Wide-eyed, the woman told the passers-by that a blast of frozen air had hit her with a force that knocked her backwards, a statement, once again, greeted by consternation or amusement by the various onlookers, depending on what type of person they were. It might have been the last gasp of a creature settling back to rest, for nothing else out of the ordinary seemed to happen around Mackenzie's tomb. Or it might have been the yawn of something finally resigning itself to waking.

A month later the same bittersweet smell and intense cold was reported in another tomb, this time inside the walled section of the Covenanters' Prison. Though the tomb had no connection with the vault of George Mackenzie, it seemed to generate the same unease. Sometimes a rapping sound coming from the interior would startle passing visitors. The tomb had an iron gate which had once been sealed, though the padlock had now vanished, and it was plain to see that there was nothing inside to make any such noise. Visitors, however, preferred to look into the darkness beyond the gate rather than enter, for the centre of the tomb seemed unnaturally cold, far more so than similar vaults further down the Covenanters' Prison. One family spotted their child giggling at the entrance to the tomb in response to 'laughing noises' he had heard coming from inside. Another young boy told his mother he had heard 'something breathing' in the darkness of the vault. Nausea and a feeling of intense cold, Alaisdair had heard, had even overcome a church member as he walked past the tomb.

Ben stood up. The shadow of the church had reached them again.

'Could you show me this vault?'

'Aye. It's right over here.'

Alaisdair rose, towering a good five inches over Ben, and strode off across the grass. He lit a cigarette as he walked, blowing a puff of smoke in the direction of George Mackenzie's ugly, squat edifice.

'Did you know,' he continued, 'there are so many bodies in here that sometimes bits of them start to stick out of the ground. Did you know that?'

He pulled Ben to the side, where a small, worn headstone leaned dispiritedly against a larger neighbour.

'See? Look at that sticking out of the ground, there. Yup. I think it's a shinbone. Now wouldn't something like that be spooky at night?'

'What do you mean, at night? It's giving me the creeps in broad daylight.'

'Aye. But things always seem a lot worse in the dark,' said Alaisdair, in a burst of philosophical musing. 'You know? At night?'

'I couldn't agree more.'

Then they were at the gates of the Covenanters' Prison. Ben pushed at the iron bars but they didn't move.

'It's locked. I don't remember it ever having been locked before.'

'It's shut all the time now. Been that way for about a month.'

'What for?'

'Edinburgh Council say there's been damage to some of the tombs in there. At least . . . that's the reason they've given.'

Alaisdair shrugged, putting a world of doubt into the gesture – as if Edinburgh Council, like God, moved in mysterious ways.

'Seems a bit of a coincidence, doesn't it?'

Ben pressed his head against the bars of the gate trying to take in as much as possible. The Covenanters' Prison was one long, green passageway about 100 yards long and 20 yards wide, bordered by a high stone wall lined with mausoleums.

'So which tomb is causing all the trouble?'

Alaisdair pointed.

'That one.'

It was as square, plain and unassuming as an eighteenth-century bus shelter, looking no different from the vaults opposite or on either side, although it was one of the few to have a roof rather than being open to the elements.

'Who's buried there?'

Alaisdair shook his head.

'Beats me. It's just a family tomb. Nobody famous, I don't think.'

He shrugged again.

'It's just a wee black mausoleum.'

'Black Mausoleum. I like that.'

Alaisdair looked at his watch.

'Listen, I better shoot off. You should think about what I said. About the tours.'

Ben shook his hand.

'I will,' he said. 'I certainly will.'

A few weeks later Edinburgh Council granted Ben Scott permission to take the newly formed 'City of the Dead' walking tour into Greyfriars graveyard. They also provided him with a set of keys to the Covenanters' Prison – once he had proved to them that his nightly walk was going to be comprehensively insured.

Elizabeth

Elizabeth Richardson had been on a City of the Dead Tour in March 2000. She rang a few days later to say that her eye was bloodshot and bruised. She appeared on the *Heaven and Earth Show* on BBC 1 in April 2000. This short interview was the only one she ever gave.

> I was standing in a corner behind someone who was six feet four inches tall. I was well out of the way and nothing had touched me at all. It wasn't until I got home that my daughter-in-law said, 'What have you done to your eye?'
>
> I looked in the mirror and it was completely red. After a couple of days I went to the doctor because it didn't go away. It was still totally red and the doctor asked me if I had knocked it or anything like that. I hadn't.

[Interviewer: So, do you think you were attacked by a ghost?]

> I would call myself fairly sceptical. I like things to be proved. But I wouldn't go back there. I wouldn't go back at night, certainly.
>
> I wouldn't do it again.

The Covenanters' Prison

On arriving at the top of the ladder with great firmness,
His heroic appearance greatly did the bystanders impress
Then Montrose asked the executioner how long his body would
    be suspended
Three hours was the answer, but Montrose was not the least
    offended.

FROM 'THE EXECUTION OF JAMES GRAHAM, MARQUIS OF MONTROSE', BY WILLIAM
    McGONAGALL

In Greyfriars Churchyard, home to the mysterious Mackenzie
Poltergeist, the number of reported encounters has
dramatically increased.

BIG ISSUE MAGAZINE, SEPTEMBER 1999

In 1560, as Greyfriars was beginning the transition from garden
to cemetery, Scotland was undergoing an equally fundamental
transformation. The nation held strong ties with Catholic
France, but their Gallic neighbours had become increasingly
overbearing, while many in lowland Scotland were gripped by
a religious fervour which was violently anti-Catholic. This new
movement was called 'Presbyterianism' – a plain, democratic
system of worship with no secular head.

As the alliance with France soured, Scotland's ties with her
old enemy, England, grew stronger, their ancient antagonism
weakened by the fact that the English were now as anti-
Catholic as the lowland Scots. This new chumminess was
cemented in 1603, when James VI of Scotland inherited the
English throne and became James I of Britain. While the
Scots rejoiced at finally conquering their long-standing

rivals, James took off for London and never came back.

This wasn't too surprising. Being cold, poverty-stricken, violent and full of religious fanatics, Scotland wasn't exactly a medieval Shangri-la. But this is how the minds of men work – they take their own flaws, warp them into something they can call virtue and use faith to tip the scales from fantasy into reality. Since Scotland was not a world player in any other department, its population used religious obsession as a lever to greatness, elevating the church to dizzy heights by presenting it as the God-given example to the rest of humanity.

The Scots began to believe that they and they alone had a special covenant with God.

At this time there was a great difference between the Scottish and English churches. Though both were Protestant and anti-Catholic, the Episcopalian Church of England was a reformed Catholic Church, with the king replacing the Pope as its head. Presbyterianism was a different matter. The Church of Scotland was fiercely autonomous, had no figurehead and had wiped all traces of 'Popery' from its kirks. To consolidate his unique and possibly precarious position as first-ever British monarch, James VI and I decided to stamp his authority on Scotland and England by whittling away the distinctions between them. Since Scotland was the smaller and poorer of the two countries, it was the one picked for a national makeover. The king's first move was to try replacing Presbyterianism with Episcopalianism, a crafty ploy which would make him head of the Church all over Britain. The Scots weren't having that; they felt that Episcopalianism was the first step to Catholicism being reintroduced into Scotland and they made no bones about how ticked-off they were. James quietly backed off and, when he died in 1625, he had made little headway in disestablishing Presbyterianism.

His son, Charles I, was a different kettle of fish. Charles was openly Catholic and, convinced of his absolute right to rule, immediately tried to force Scotland to accept his father's religious changes. The lowland Scots had remained loyal to a long line of Stuart kings, despite some of these monarchs' spectacular shortcomings, but Charles I had gone too far. You just didn't mess with Scottish religion.

Pressure came to a head when, on 23 July 1637, an Episcopalian prayer book was read out at St Giles' Cathedral, Edinburgh. A riot ensued which quickly escalated into a rebellion. Leading Presbyterians drew up the 'National Covenant', a 'mission statement' outlining the goals of their movement. It was an impressively long-winded document, but its message was clear and threatening: the Scots would remain loyal to Charles I only if he stopped trying to impose Episcopalianism on them. If he did not, they would fight him.

On 8 December 1638 the National Covenant was signed in Greyfriars Church, Edinburgh, witnessed by representatives from all over the country. In those days, Greyfriars churchyard still had plenty of room for bodies and the headstones were few and simple, but it is said the emerald slopes of the cemetery were obscured by 60,000 spectators. As the Covenant was read aloud to the multitudes, every right hand was raised as the crowd swore a sacred oath to uphold and defend its contents. Hour after hour nobles, tradesmen and peasants filed through the church of Greyfriars, signing copies. Some wrote 'till death' after their names. Others signed in blood rather than ink. Copies were dispatched around the country to be signed in towns, villages and homesteads. By the end of the year (with the exception of the Catholic Highlands) Scotland was fully Presbyterian.

For a change, these 'Covenanters' stressed that they had no quarrel with the English and only wanted their religion left alone, and they found sympathy in England, where many considered Charles far too Popish and tyrannical for their liking. After losing a series of battles to the Covenanters and facing a rebellion on his own doorstep, Charles agreed the Scots could have all the concessions they wanted.

It was a case of too little too late. In 1642, the English Civil War broke out and the more resolute Covenanters felt they could turn this situation to their advantage. They negotiated a treaty with Oliver Cromwell, leader of the southern rebellion, and his English Parliament. This second document, the Solemn League and Covenant, offered military help to Cromwell in return for Scottish Presbyterianism being established, not just in Scotland, but throughout the whole of Britain. It was an ambitious, over-zealous move and it spelt doom for the Covenanters. Charles had already given the Scots the religious concessions they wanted and many Covenanting nobles thought they were now going back on their word. Feeling he had betrayed his king, the Marquis of Montrose – one of the main Covenanter leaders – switched sides and began a Royalist insurrection in Scotland. Leading a small band of Irish Catholics and Highlanders, he scored six successive victories over his former allies until he was betrayed, defeated and beheaded outside St Giles' Cathedral.

Although Montrose was beaten, the Covenanters were baffled by what had happened. How could they lose battles? They were God's soldiers, for God's sake! Yet they had never become a decisive military presence in England either and, as Charles neared total defeat, the English parliament refused to honour the Presbyterian demands. Crippled by English betrayal and inner divisions, the Covenanting movement began to collapse.

Then, in 1650, Oliver Cromwell and the English parliament executed the captured Charles I, to the horror of even the staunchest of Presbyterians. The Stuarts were an ancient line of Scottish kings and the English couldn't go around chopping their heads off, no matter what they had done. The new Covenanter leader, Argyll, immediately crowned the beheaded monarch's son, Charles II, though he kept the young king a virtual prisoner while the Covenanters moulded him into a good Presbyterian. Cromwell retaliated by occupying Scotland and forcing Charles into nine years of exile.

Oliver Cromwell died in 1660. He had turned out to be far too puritanical for the British population, who were happy to re-establish the monarchy before they expired of boredom. Charles II, determined never to be a pawn again, immediately had Argyll executed and set about destroying what was left of the Covenanting movement. Secure in a position of power his father and grandfather had never enjoyed, Charles II (also a secret Catholic) forcibly brought Episcopalianism back to Scotland. He outlawed the once proud Covenanters, who were now forced to hold their religious services in hiding or at remote locations. But they were not yet defeated. In 1672 they murdered the Archbishop of St Andrews, a defector from the Presbyterian side to the Episcopalian one, defeated Royal troops at the Battle of Drumclog and began to assemble for one last desperate battle at Bothwell Bridge, on the River Clyde.

The Covenanters didn't stand a chance. They were outnumbered, ill-disciplined, bickering amongst themselves and poorly armed and equipped. In the ensuing rout 400 Presbyterians died and around 1,200 were taken prisoner. They were bound two by two and dragged the breadth of Scotland to Edinburgh, where they were greeted by mobs jeering 'Where's your God now?'

Edinburgh council faced a unique problem. There were suddenly 1,200 prisoners crammed into a city which was one of the most overcrowded in Europe. Also, Edinburgh wasn't exactly the hub of polite civilisation – the city jails were already filled to overflowing. The official solution was effective, if typically savage; the prisoners were herded into Greyfriars churchyard and locked in the south-west section. There was no shelter in this large walled yard, not even a covering to keep out the rain, and yet they were held there for five months. Penned like animals, the Covenanters slept on the cold winter ground and snipers were posted to shoot any of them heard moving around at night. They were poorly fed and forbidden contact with any friends in the city who might dare show them comfort.

As the months passed, the number of prisoners decreased. Some were set loose after giving a pledge that they would never bear arms against their king again. A few of the luckier, or more resourceful, prisoners escaped by befriending the guards or climbing over the graveyard wall. The less fortunate ones succumbed to the elements, hunger or disease and died where they lay. By mid-November there were only 257 occupants left in what had become known as the 'Covenanters' Prison' – and their misery, if it were possible, was about to increase.

Early one morning they were marched from Greyfriars graveyard to Leith docks, where a ship named the *Crown* awaited them; the Privy Council of Edinburgh had decided that the remaining Covenanters were to be deported to the West Indies and sold as slaves. All 257 unfortunate souls were crammed into a stinking, black hold not large enough to hold 100 men. Those who were well enough stood to allow the sick and dying the last poor solace of lying on the rough deck floor. Their meat was tainted and fresh water was scarce. One Covenanter, James Corson, wrote to his wife:

> All the troubles we met since Bothwell were not to be compared to one day in our present circumstances. Our uneasiness is beyond words. Yet the consolations of God overbalance all: and I hope we are near our port and heaven is open for us.

He was a lot closer to heaven than he realised. Off the coast of Orkney the *Crown* ran into a massive storm. The captain fastened chains over the hatches that held the terrified, vomiting prisoners and tried to reach calmer waters closer to shore.

He miscalculated. At ten o'clock the jagged rocks off the Orkney shore loomed out of the darkness and the ship broke its back on them. The sailors toppled the mast over the side and used it like a bridge to reach the beach but the Covenanters, locked in the darkness of the flooded hold, could not follow. Fewer than sixty managed to reach the safety of the shore as the *Crown* shattered into pieces. The other 200 vanished into the black waters.

It seemed the Covenanters' God had finally deserted them.

The tattered remnants of the once powerful movement were now hunted men and the 18 years that followed became known as the 'Killing Times'. Though the exact figure will never be known, it is estimated that 18,000 men, women and even children died in a policy of ruthless intimidation that stretched the length and breadth of Scotland.

One man was responsible, more than any other, for this mass extermination – the king's Advocate in Scotland.

His name was George Mackenzie.

Rachael

Written statement by Rachael Darrow, who entered the Covenanters' Prison on 1 September 2000:

My name is Rachael Darrow and I grew up in Janesville, Wisconsin, USA. Currently I am in college at the University of Wisconsin-Eau Claire studying psychology and plan to attend graduate school to gain a PhD in counselling. I am 21 years old and was studying in England when my experience happened.

I went on a night tour to Greyfriars graveyard with friends. In the Covenanters' Prison I felt extremely faint and started breathing rapidly. I do not get scared easily, so I don't know why I had this reaction. While we were walking toward the tomb [the Black Mausoleum] which we were all going to enter, I felt as if it were suddenly getting colder. I did not think much of it, because it was a chilly night, but as soon as we entered the room I began to shake uncontrollably. I ended up having to brace myself against the wall, shaking and hyperventilating – I felt I could not breathe properly. I felt better the moment we were allowed to leave the area. This was a very strange thing to happen to me because I have never fainted in my life and have never felt that way before or since.

The next day I had a welt above my left eye which did not go away for about two weeks.

The experience will stay with me forever.

'Bloody' George

The mausoleum in which he lies in the Greyfriars Churchyard, a domed edifice with ornate Corinthian columns and niches, is believed by the urchins of the city to be haunted still, as it was commonly believed that his body could never rest in its grave. Hence it used to be deemed a 'brag' or feat, for a boy more courageous than his fellows to shout through the keyhole into the dark and echoing tomb,

> 'Bluidy Mackenzie, come out if ye daur,
> Lift the sneck, and draw the bar!'

after which defiance all fled, lest the summoned spirit might appear, and follow them.

JAMES GRANT, *CASSELL'S OLD AND NEW EDINBURGH* (1880–1883)

Greyfriars is the most haunted place you'll find in Edinburgh.

HUGH WILLIAMS, RADIO 1, APRIL 2000

For a man who gained notoriety persecuting Covenanters, George Mackenzie had a rather surprising past. Before becoming Charles II's Advocate in Scotland, Mackenzie had actually shown great zeal in defending the very movement he ended up destroying. When the Covenanter leader, the Marquis of Argyll, was tried for treason in 1660, Mackenzie was one of the advocates who defended him. A year later he turned up on the side of another major Covenanter, James Guthrie, and five years later fought in the courts to try to free Presbyterian prisoners taken after their defeat at the battle of Rullion Green.

Born in Dundee in 1636, George Mackenzie was educated at Kings College, Aberdeen, and proved to be an intelligent and liberal thinker. He wrote many acclaimed legal texts, challenged the ignorant persecution of so-called witches and founded the Advocates Library, which eventually became the National Library of Scotland. But George Mackenzie was an aristocrat and an Episcopalian, accepting the divine right of the Stuart kings and believing that the Covenanters were dangerous and wrong. Once properly established in his profession, it was no longer necessary for Mackenzie to show off his skills by defending the Presbyterian movement.

It was at this point that the strange transformation of George Mackenzie began. He turned to speaking out against the Covenanters and eventually began persecuting them. By the time he became Lord Advocate of Scotland in 1677, Mackenzie's fervour had transformed into obsession, and he had changed from a compassionate liberal to a tyrant who fervently sought the destruction of the Presbyterian movement.

Mackenzie formed a cruel alliance with the military commander John Graham of Claverhouse. Mackenzie condemned the Covenanters from the judges' bench, using every official trick he knew and resorting to torture or duplicity whenever his legal channels failed. Claverhouse carried out the dirty work, hunting down and executing Covenanters in the field and earning himself the nickname 'Bluidy Clavers' to match the gory moniker of his partner in crime. It is ironic that history records Mackenzie as metamorphosing from a liberal into a monster, for Claverhouse would undergo a reverse transformation, eventually becoming famous as the heroic 'Bonnie Dundee'. Between 1684 and 1688, however, the atrocities committed towards the Covenanters by Claverhouse and Mackenzie reached a horrific peak – this period became known as the 'Killing Times'. Presbyterians were hunted down by men with bloodhounds, spies were hired to join their numbers then betray them and soldiers had permission to shoot on the spot anyone refusing to swear allegiance to the king. Yet such was the power of their faith that many Covenanters, men and women, died rather than betray their convictions.

In 1685, Charles II died and was succeeded by his brother James Stuart. James VII had no more love for Presbyterianism than his brother but while Charles II had been secretly Catholic, James reopened old wounds in Britain by admitting to his Catholic beliefs and pushing for more religious tolerance. It seemed a decent thing on the surface but aroused the fury of a nation who saw just what James was up to. More religious tolerance for everybody meant more religious tolerance for Catholics, whose fortunes at this point in British history had sunk so low that they could not even hold any positions of office. If all religions were allowed equal rights, James could begin to put his Catholic friends into influential posts once more – and everyone knew it.

Presbyterians were still hounded by the king's men and shunned, through fear or ignorance, by the rest of the Scots, but no group aroused hatred like the Catholics. Though the persecution of the Covenanters carried blithely on, Catholics in Scotland, protected by James VII, began to flourish. Catholic schools were established, popish ecclesiasticals brought in from the continent and honours bestowed on men who sought the king's favour by suddenly declaring that they'd actually been Catholics all along.

It was the end of the road for the 'bluidy' double act of Mackenzie and Claverhouse. George Mackenzie resigned in disgust at the new royal policy while John Graham stayed loyal to his king. When James VII was deposed because of his beliefs, Claverhouse earned his place in Scots legend by giving his life in a doomed attempt to put the exiled monarch back on the throne.

James VII's successor, William, would have been quite happy to maintain Episcopalianism in Scotland, but a great deal of the Episcopal clergy there had been appointed by, and remained loyal to, James. The simplest way to get rid of them was to restore Presbyterianism to Scotland – and that's just what William did.

After over half a century of fighting, Presbyterianism was handed to Scotland on a plate. It was just a shame there were hardly any Covenanters left to celebrate the fact.

Sir George Mackenzie lived long enough to witness his great crusade grind to a shuddering halt. With his career in ruins, he spent his last night in Scotland sitting amongst the graves in Greyfriars cemetery lamenting his fate. He died in 1691, just in time to see the Stuart line end and Presbyterianism become the religion of his country. He was buried in a great mausoleum in Greyfriars, probably the most imposing vault in the cemetery, right next to the Covenanters' Prison and just yards from where the National Covenant was signed. Close to his tomb is the headstone of his mortal enemy, Alexander Henderson, the minister who drew up the National Covenant. (On close inspection visitors can still find musket-ball holes from the days when the king's troops would use his headstone for target practice.) Farther down the hill, against the graveyard wall, is the 'Martyr's Monument', celebrating the bravery of those Mackenzie destroyed. The inscription on the monument reads:

> From May 27th 1661 that the noble Marquess of Argyle suffered to the 17th of Febr. 1688 that Mr James Ranwick suffered, were executed at Edinburgh about a hundred of Noble Gentlemen Ministers & others noble martyres for JESUS CHRIST.
> The most part of them lie here.

The Covenanter's story may have ended in Greyfriars graveyard, but George Mackenzie's legend did not. As the years passed, tales of strange occurrences happening around his dark and sinister tomb began to circulate. Greyfriars was to be the site of as much horror in the future as it had seen in its Covenanting past, causing its haunted reputation to grow with the centuries.

The first weight had been added to the balance. It would shift Greyfriars graveyard from a place of eternal rest to a site where the dead refused to lie still.

Jan

Written statement by Jan Adamson-Reese, who was in Greyfriars Churchyard on the night of 20 May 2000:

How would you react if someone told you they'd had a paranormal experience? Would you be sceptical? Gasp in horror? Laugh uproariously? Think it was a load of old codswallop? If someone had asked me the same question 12 months ago, I'd have made interested noises at the time and had a good giggle afterwards. But something happened to me in May 2000 which changed all that . . .

The tour began outside St Giles' Cathedral on the Royal Mile at 10 p.m., and there I was, tagging along with a crowd of 30 holidaymakers and tourists of all ages and nationalities, preparing to be led round the back streets of Edinburgh on a historical tour which culminated with a visit to Greyfriars Kirkyard.

As we drew nearer the flight of steps leading up to the ancient kirkyard, the tour guide, Ben, asked for our attention and advised us that we were entering the graveyard at our own risk . . . that he could in no way be held responsible for any eventualities and that we were at liberty to back out at that point if we wished to do so. The whispers started up immediately: 'Do you think anything'll happen?', 'Oh, my God, it's so scary', 'Are we gonna go through with this?' I've got to say I found it all highly amusing.

As we mounted the dark steps leading into the graveyard, the 30-strong crowd became strangely silent and moved closer together, away from the shadows. At the other side of the graveyard lay the Covenanters' Prison, kept locked day and night with a heavy chain and padlock. I had heard stories about the existence of a poltergeist, and read newspaper articles about individuals who had been attacked or experienced some other inexplicable sensation. I was also giggling like mad, because a large number of people were getting extremely nervous. Couldn't they see that the entire thing was a huge charade, a complete fabrication, dreamed up to con unsuspecting tourists???

The guide swung the heavy iron gates aside to let us through. Was it my imagination, or did the air become distinctly chilly as we walked into the prison? Good grief, I was getting as bad as the rest of them!

The deeper we were led into the prison, the quieter everyone became. We stopped outside the Black Mausoleum, the crowd huddling together. I was standing at the edge of the group, a little apart from the others. The guide began to speak. At that moment, I felt the oddest sensation on the back of my head – a light, cold sensation, as though someone was tracing a pattern on my scalp with one finger. Instinctively, I turned round. There was no one standing beside me, no one within arm's reach. I touched my scalp. Weird! No trees around either, so it couldn't have been a branch. I was unsettled, but not overly concerned.

Then we were led into the tomb itself. It was pitch black, with a faint, musty smell. As we huddled together at the back of the tomb, listening to what the guide was saying, all of a sudden I felt violently sick . . . I could feel the nausea rising in my throat and it took a tremendous effort to remain standing upright. I was convinced I was either going to faint or throw up all over the backpacker standing in front of me. This intense wave of nausea continued for a minute or two. I was fighting it the entire time, but once we were led out of the tomb again into the cool night air, I felt instantly better.

But something wasn't quite right.

Putting my hands up to touch my face, I realised with a shock that I had lost all feeling there. It was as though I had received a particularly effective anaesthetic at the dentist, numbing it completely. The rest of my body was at normal temperature, but my face was stone cold. This feeling lasted, incredibly, for almost half an hour.

I have been back to Greyfriars on a number of occasions since, even taking part in a couple of television interviews about the poltergeist there. One film crew wanted to interview me standing in the tomb, and it proved very unsettling, as I was affected in exactly the same way – my face grew cold and lost all sensation. I'm afraid I didn't stay there much longer.

On another occasion, the morning after I'd taken part in an interview in the churchyard, I woke to find three red marks on my skin, two on my abdomen and one on my leg. They resembled burns but were not painful. All had disappeared within 24 hours.

Mackenzie Mark I

People complained of mysterious attacks. They reported being bitten or scratched or having their hair pulled when no one else seemed to be around. Some felt strangely cold on warm days, while others reported that fires started for no apparent reason. Now an American Paranormal expert believes Mackenzie was to blame for these incidents – and that he has returned with a vengeance after three years . . .

Parapsychologist R.D. Slaither noticed activity similar to that previously experienced in the Niddry Street vaults in the Covenanters' Prison next to Mackenzie's grave in Greyfriars Kirkyard.

'Is this graveyard the home of Edinburgh's scariest poltergeist?'

EDINBURGH EVENING NEWS, 3 JULY 1999

It has the reputation of being the most haunted spot in the most haunted city in Britain. And now that I stand here, it's extremely spooky and very atmospheric. 100 per cent belief.

ROSS KELLY, *GOOD MORNING TELEVISION,* MARCH 2000

Edinburgh has quite a reputation. It's beautiful city – one of the most breathtaking in Europe – but it is also a city of duality, of dark and hidden things. The cramped and gnarled aspect of the medieval Old Town looms over the spacious Georgian New Town. Conservationists war with developers over whether a twelfth-century castle is more attractive to visitors than a Harvey Nicks. As the tourist capital of Scotland, the city extends the hand of friendship to visitors across the globe – but homegrown louts, safe in their numbers and drunk on their own warped nationalism, still chant racist slogans from the darkness at passers-by whose accents do not match their own.

The heart of this glory and decay is the Old Town, where hidden bridges and sudden drops mangle the narrow streets, making it easy to lose oneself even in that tiny twisted area. It is Edinburgh's black heart, and it certainly seems to have more than its fair share of ghosts. There are reasons for this. For one thing, the Old Town retains enough of its historic visage to give a good idea of what it looked like in past centuries. In fact, many of the buildings pull off their 'ancient' look simply by being grubby and oddly shaped. They fire the imagination anyway.

The Old Town has a long and gory history. It pretty much was Edinburgh for many centuries and remained medieval long after the rest of the continent had cleaned up its act. For over 200 years Edinburgh was also one of the most overcrowded cities in Europe. Life in the capital was very cheap, and death was frequent and bloody.

In the summer the city is crammed with foreign visitors who want history, now, and lots of it. The best way to bring that history to life is to have it hanging around, even after the developers have had their way. If an ale house frequented by Black Dugald McNasty has been turned into a theme bar, there's no reason why Black Dugald himself can't still pop up now and then to haunt the ladies' toilet – it gives the place a bit of historical context at a fraction of the price it would cost to preserve the original building. A particularly popular ghost can be wide-ranging, allowing different establishments to gain from the benefit of its presence. A little drummer boy, for instance, is supposed to haunt a hidden passage running the length of the Royal Mile, which gives him licence to spice up just about any premise he wants.

The Old Town, if the stories are to be believed, is positively overrun with supernatural denizens. In a space a mile long and less than a few hundred yards wide you can encounter the phantom piper, the phantom bloodstain, the Watcher, the phantom marchers, the phantom drummer, the headless drummer, the ghost of Mrs Guthrie, the death coach, the white lady, little Sarah, the Wizard of the West Bow, Shadowjack Henry, the kitchen boy of Queensbury house, The Imp, The Ghost of Holyrood Palace, the spectre of Ramsay Gardens, and the unfortunately named Hanged Horace.

With more spirits than a Polish vodka bar, the fact that you don't see an Old Town Ghost on any particular day would seem to be a talking point. But the Royal Mile ghosts have the same elusive quality as its parking spaces – there are always thousands of people on the lookout, but nobody ever spots one. In the past, this didn't seem to be the case. The Victorians, for instance, couldn't get five minutes' peace without falling over a ghost. So what has changed? Have all the spectres left town?

The truth is that ghost stories, like all good tales, grow grander with each telling until the truth is only a small thread in the fabric of their tapestry. In the Old Town, the famous 'ghosts' of Mary King's Close, for instance, owe their existence to a book called *Satan's Invisible World*, published in 1685 by George Sinclair, Professor of Moral Philosophy at Glasgow University. This medieval bestseller painted the unfortunate street as a hotbed of supernatural activity and it retains that reputation. The fact that Sinclair made the whole thing up has been conveniently forgotten.

As the centuries march on and science claims a tighter and tighter hold on the beliefs of the Western world, the number of new ghosts grows smaller. Edinburgh may have more than its fair share of spooks, but then Edinburgh has more than its fair share of heavy drinkers. Even the tourists are no longer as gullible. A 1990 Gallup poll of adult Americans showed that only 35 per cent believed in ghosts – roughly the same percentage as those who believed in the lost continent of Atlantis, and about half those who believed in Noah's flood.

Occasionally, however, a new phantom in town causes a flicker of doubt among the sceptics. In 1957 the 'Hazeldean Poltergeist' hit the headlines of the Edinburgh newspapers. That spring, No. 5 Hazeldean Terrace seemed to have become a focus for poltergeist activity. A wooden chopping board was frequently propelled across the room, mugs and cups broke in two and the family were kept awake by unexplained banging noises coming from the kitchen. The phenomenon lasted about two years before tailing off but attracted nationwide media attention at the time.

In Niddry Street, Edinburgh, in 1994, there appeared to be another spate of poltergeist activity. Niddry Street is a short, narrow thoroughfare dipping steeply from Edinburgh's Royal Mile into the Cowgate. On one side is the impressive presence of the Crowne Plaza Hotel, while the other side of the street contains decaying tenements and is dotted with nightclubs, pubs and old bridge vaults. In the past, Niddry Street had the usual hotch-potch of ghosts boasted by every ancient wynd in Edinburgh. A featureless man in a frock coat was often seen in one of the pubs – surely a new use for the term 'off your face' – the hotel had a reputation for 'strange occurrences' and the hostel next door had a ghost in the laundry room. None of this was out of the ordinary in the Old Town. Just round the corner was the ghost of a woman knifed to death in 1916 and a bunch of spectral children who died in the plague of 1645. But between 1994 and 1996, Niddry Street seemed to be haunted by an entity that was different from the run-of-the-mill spooks. People in the street complained of inexplicable drops in temperature. The area was plagued by fires. Passers-by felt nauseous or suddenly terrified for no apparent reason; some even collapsed. These events were strikingly similar to those that would take place in Greyfriars Graveyard five years later. Was there some connection?

Perhaps there was more than one.

Ben Scott was working as a tour guide at that time and his walk began and ended each night in Niddry Street. He bade goodnight to his party outside a pub that employed a young barman named David Pollock. David Pollock had never heard of the Mackenzie Poltergeist and would not for a few more years. But his life and the life of the poltergeist would become entwined in a way he could not have imagined.

In 1996, Ben Scott stopped taking tours into Niddry Street and David Pollock moved to another bar in another street. When they did, the paranormal occurrences in Niddry Street faded away. There were no more cold spots. Nobody collapsed. The poltergeist, if that was indeed what it was, had gone.

And the third connection? The Crowne Plaza was built on the site of Strichen's Close, another victim of twentieth-century developers after surviving for half a millennium.

Strichen's Close had been the home of the illustrious George Mackenzie.

Kyle

Statement given by Kyle Plackmeyer from Maryville, Missouri, a radio operator on a cruise ship. Mr Plackmeyer encountered the Mackenzie Poltergeist on 14 July 2000.

When it is possible to explain away an incident by natural, or sometimes clever human, origins, I do my best to do so. I took the City of the Dead tour after exhausting the other 'ghost tours' of Edinburgh. I saw Mary King's Close and some of the other reported haunted places and did not register anything. The cemetery tour was the second to last night of my week vacation before I went to the Open at St Andrews and then back to the cruise ship I work on. I expected only a good story then maybe a night in the pub. I did not drink beforehand though and I was in the mindset for light-hearted fun, not sombreness.

The tour gave a wonderful account of Edinburgh's gritty past and the excitement mounted as we neared Greyfriars. I felt a tinge of anticipation that something might happen, but it was in the back of my mind for the most part. The stories continued as we entered the mausoleum which is reported to be the active area. Our guide continued speaking and I was in what I would call starboard aft of the structure, if you don't mind nautical terminology.

My incident occurred about one or two minutes after entering. I stood listening at the back of the crowd when, without hearing voices or any of the other phenomena reported, I felt something I have never encountered before. Hopefully, I will never feel it again. It was akin to having someone wrap a black cloak of ice around me. It was hard to breathe and became *very* cold, *very* quickly. It was not like a breeze though. The air was quite still and just dropped dramatically. I began to black out. I remembered the guide's advice that if something strange happened, to move. I tried to step away, but continued to feel frozen and unable to draw a breath, like a deer in headlights, totally fixed in place. I finally forced myself to jump. Though it only took about four seconds or so for the entire ordeal, it passed slowly, and I recall vividly the sickening feeling in my stomach.

Out of the entire group, only the lady standing next to me looked at me. Maybe she thought I was trying to be cute with an attempt at scaring everyone by a sudden movement. I only wish that to be true. I'm not sure if the guide noticed or if he just let it go without trying to shake everyone else up. Usually cool-headed, I now had an acute case of the shakes. I wanted to leave but honestly was too frightened to move without the rest of the group. As the tour ended, many people went together to a nearby pub, which was my original intent of my evening. I passed on this, went back to my lodgings and had a hard time falling asleep without reflecting on the evening.

The next morning, I saw the guide walking down the street. I told him my story and also told him that I had said nothing the previous evening because I did not want to stop until I was well away from the activity's location. He gave me the company's phone number and I subsequently gave them my story and address.

Dawn of The Dead

Elaine Weyman, 34, an administrator for a large insurance company, claimed she had been attacked by the ghost three weeks ago. Although she only felt 'chilly' in the tomb, when she woke up next day she had bruising around her neck — as if 'something' had grabbed her from behind.

'Tourists feel force of phantom menace'
EDINBURGH EVENING NEWS, 6 NOVEMBER 1999

Ben Scott sat in Bannerman's Bar with his friends, many of whom were also guides. He had decided to wait until they had drunk a significant amount before springing his idea on them.

'Listen. I'm starting a walking tour. A ghost tour. Who wants to come? All we need is a little money to start off . . .'

His enthusiasm was not reciprocated. The other guides knew that Edinburgh already had plenty of ghost tours. It didn't need another one.

'But we'll be better than the competition. I'm good at this.'

His friends didn't disagree. Ben knew how to tell a story. The problem was that the competition was too big for any small company to even get a foothold. Ben tried his *pièce de résistance*.

'Ah. But I've got a real ghost. Apparently.'

His friends shook their heads.

'Aye,' Ben agreed. 'That sounded stupid, even to me.'

Ben's ex-girlfriend Kate Kavanagh, also a tour guide, was sitting at his right-hand side. At 27, Kate was ten years younger than Ben and several inches shorter. While Ben's accent had a soft, almost imperceptible, Scottish lilt, Kate had a broad Yorkshire accent. Slim, with shoulder-length auburn hair, Kate was striking and fiery-tempered. Deep in conversation with the girl across the table, she hadn't appeared to be listening. Now she turned and lit a cigarette.

'How much are we talking about?'

Ben spun round to face her.

'Not much. Money to make a few signs advertising the tour. Cash to print some leaflets. What else do we need?'

'A miracle,' someone suggested.

'I've got some money,' Kate said, and turned back to her conversation.

'There,' said Ben. 'That's miracle number one. Who wants a drink? It's my round.'

'That's miracle number two!'

The dire predictions almost came true – the newly formed City of the Dead tour didn't exactly make an immediate impact. People enjoyed the historical stories and laughed at the jokes. Ben knew how to write a good script, both he and Kate knew how to give a performance and Greyfriars was suitably forbidding at night. But, as their friends had frequently commented, there were plenty of similarly themed tours in Edinburgh – the bigger companies, regardless of how good they were, could afford mass advertising and had cornered the market.

Then Kate met R.D. Slaither.

It was a grey day, despite being June, and the cemetery looked like it was filtered through monochrome or, perhaps, turning to dust. Kate had gone to the Covenanters' Prison to put a new padlock on the Black Mausoleum as the old one seemed to have vanished. She didn't like the Covenanters' Prison. Ben strolled in and out of the place quite happily, but Kate was reluctant to enter it even during the day. It wasn't so much the fear factor, though it was certainly scary at night. It was more that the small strip of land seemed to carry an air of sadness. It was a melancholy place, like Glencoe or Culloden, a place where the atrocities carried out many years ago seemed to linger. Ben felt none of this and had remarked several times that it would be a great spot to have a picnic.

Kate was locking the gate behind her when she heard a movement to her left and a dark shape flitted into the corner of her eye.

'Jesus Christ Almighty!' Dragging the chain from the gate, she whirled to face the intruder with a speed that would have impressed Bruce Lee.

A tall, white-haired man stood in front of her, hands in pockets. He was dressed casually but smartly and had the air of a man who knew how to wear clothes well. His face was tanned and wrinkled, but it was a face that wore the mark of travel rather than age. Kate was sure she recognised him.

'I don't know if you recognise me,' the man smiled disarmingly. 'I was on your tour last night.' His accent was odd; it seemed to be a mixture of Scots and American. 'Name's R.D. Slaither.' The man held out his hand. 'I wondered if I might have a word with you.'

Kate looked around to see if there was anyone else in the graveyard and was relieved to see a couple walking arm in arm less than 100 yards away. She relaxed her grip on the chain and shook R.D. Slaither's hand.

'What can I do for you?'

'I'm a parapsychologist,' said Slaither. Kate tightened her grip on the chain again.

'Don't worry,' said Slaither. 'I'm not loopy. I investigate so-called psychic phenomena, true, but I think most of it is fake, or has a valid scientific explanation. Still . . . that's what I'm interested in. I came on your tour last night.'

'You're investigating our tour?'

Slaither smiled. He had an open, likeable smile.

'Hell no. I'm here for the weekend – I just had nothing better to do. But I wanted to ask you about something.'

'What would you like to know?' Kate sat on one of the stone grave borders and felt for her cigarettes.

'How long have these tours been going?'

'Not long. About a month. Month and a half.'

'Do people get scared?'

'Well, yes. It's a ghost tour.'

'Yes. I enjoyed it.'

Slaither sat on the border beside her.

'You ever heard of a thin place?'

Kate looked blank, puzzled by his sudden change of tack.

'No. What is it?'

'According to folklore, a thin place is a place where the dividing line between this world and – I don't know, the spirit world, call it what you like – is very thin. Balquidder, up near Callander, is supposed to be a thin place. Where Rob Roy McGregor used to live.'

Slaither looked straight ahead, as if peering into this other world, or perhaps just seeing Balquidder again.

'I went there once. I'm very good at, I don't know, "sensing" things. Call it what you like. That's why I do what I do.'

'Did you sense anything in Balquidder?'

'Hell no. Very pretty though. A lot of silver birch. Nice type of tree.'

He shook his head and laughed.

'Spirit world. No. Lot of nonsense.'

Despite Slaither's pleasant demeanour, Kate was beginning to wish she hadn't put the chain down. She looked around, but the courting couple were nowhere to be seen.

'Why do you end the tour in that tomb?'

'What tomb?'

'The tomb you end the tour in.' Slaither smiled again, but now Kate was watching his eyes. She couldn't tell whether they were friendly or not; they didn't reveal anything.

'We heard it was haunted. Thought it would be the perfect place to finish.' Kate looked around again.

'It is.'

'Yes. It's very atmospheric. You saw how scared people were.'

'I mean, yes. It is haunted. Well . . . not exactly haunted – I don't really believe in that nonsense. But you got something in there. I felt it.'

Despite her nervousness, Kate couldn't resist arching one shapely eyebrow. Slaither smiled again, and once again he seemed friendly and harmless.

'I know. Sounds dumb. Let's just say, I've been to a lot of places. I've seen a lot of so-called paranormal occurrences. Most of them were all smoke and mirrors.'

His smile faded.

'But now and then I come across something. I get this feeling. I sense something. And I have never sensed it stronger than in that tomb.'

'Is it . . . dangerous?' Kate tried to sound nonchalant.

'Hell, yes.'

Slaither stood up.

'Won't stop you dong the tours though, will it?'

Kate gave a little smile as she, too, stood. She shook her head.

'Hell no.'

Slaither stretched out his hand again.

'Good. Good. I'll be back to check on this one. Good luck.'

They shook hands once again and R.D. Slaither turned and strolled off towards the graveyard exit. Kate picked up the padlock, walked over to the gate and wrapped the chain around it. She glanced back, but by now R.D. Slaither was almost out of the main gate. For the first time she noticed he was limping.

As she clicked the padlock shut, she suddenly felt very cold.

'Jesus. It doesn't take much to give me the creeps,' she said, more to fill the sudden silence than anything else.

She never saw R.D. Slaither again.

The next week 11-year-old Megan Billingsly, visiting from Leeds, came on the City of the Dead tour. Once the walk had ended she complained to her mother that something she couldn't see had 'clawed her hand' in the Black Mausoleum.

In the light from the streetlamps the astonished tour party could see four deep gouges running across the back of her arm.

Joy

Statement by Joy Frazer who spent the summer of 2000 visiting ghost tours around the country and analysing them from a folkloristic perspective:

> Of the tours that I have studied, City of the Dead is most definitely located at the fear-inducing end of the spectrum. The company first caught my attention with its promise to offer its audiences the experience of being 'locked in a graveyard at night with an active poltergeist'. Although most ghost tours incorporate (or purport to incorporate) an experience that is in some way 'supernatural', none report such experiences with the frequency, and seriousness, of those described by participants on this company's tours.
>
> Secondly, I was interested in the emphasis placed by the tour company on the genuineness and potential harmfulness of this promised supernatural encounter. This emphasis continues throughout the tour itself; as Ben informed one tour party of which I was a member, 'Whether or not you believe in this kind of thing is now immaterial . . . [It] is real and I do warn you of that now.'
>
> A series of gates through which the tour party passes on its way to the Black Mausoleum are first unlocked to allow the audience members to pass through, and then locked again behind them, simultaneously creating the contradictory impressions of privileged access and entrapment. It is an exciting and fear-inducing combination. On one tour I attended, once his audience had crammed into the

mausoleum, Ben further reinforced the sense of entrapment by closing the gate from the outside and making as if to walk away. When this action was met with expressions of genuine alarm from his audience he returned, only to inform them that the zone in which the poltergeist was most likely to attack was also their only possible escape route; the doorway of the tomb itself.

During the summer of 2000 I attended the tour on six occasions, surely making me its greatest fan! Each time the experience became more, not less, frightening. However, for all that they use their power as intermediaries to manipulate the emotions of the audience, the guides themselves are not exempt from the dangers involved in conducting tours to the Black Mausoleum. In fact, on a tour I attended on 29 July 2000, led by another guide, it was obvious that his considerable fear was not simply part of the performance. This fear was quickly communicated to the audience, and despite his urging us to 'stay light-hearted', that we were 'here to have fun', several audience members chose to leave the tour before it entered the Covenanters' Prison and fun was the last thing on most of our minds. Speaking for myself, I have rarely been so afraid, and it seemed that our fears were not unfounded.

After the tour, I spoke with a fellow audience member, Charity Pirkle, who professed to having been 'scared half to death' by a paranormal experience on the tour. Charity's description of her experience is consistent with other accounts of noises issuing from behind the walls of the mausoleum and of bruises appearing after the tour where victims have felt the sensation of being touched.

The Ghost That Haunted Itself

Laws of nature are just human inventions, like ghosts. Laws of logic, of mathematics are also human inventions, like ghosts. The whole blessed thing is a human invention, including the idea that it isn't a human invention. The world has no existence whatsoever outside the human imagination. It's all a ghost, and in antiquity was so recognised as a ghost, the whole blessed world we live in.

ROBERT M. PIRSIG, *ZEN AND THE ART OF MOTORCYCLE MAINTENANCE*

There appears to be something very spooky going on in Greyfriars Kirkyard in Edinburgh. Many visitors have reported being jostled, scratched and generally assaulted by invisible assailants. There have been cold spots, ethereal rappings and laughter and the smell of putrefaction. Visitors have felt nauseous or even passed out.

'Ghosts gang up on the visitors to Greyfriars'
SUNDAY TELEGRAPH, 23 APRIL 2000

From the day that Kate Kavanagh met R.D. Slaither, whether it was coincidence or not, paranormal incidents seemed to come thick and fast. On 19 June 1999, Lisa Allen from Boston complained of being freezing cold while the tour party were in the Black Mausoleum. Ben Scott made several jokes about Scottish summers then watched, astonished, as the young woman fell unconscious to the ground. She woke up a few minutes later and, when questioned, insisted she had felt some kind of presence materialise next to her in the darkness immediately before she blacked out.

On 25 June 1999, Mhaile Moore from Polynesia began to

panic in the darkness of the Black Mausoleum. In front of Kate and the bemused tour party, she shouted that something was pulling her by the hair. Yet nobody was standing anywhere near her – nor did they want to after that. On 1 July 1999, a tour party led by Kate heard a rumbling noise coming from the Black Mausoleum as they walked towards it. Some visitors described it as a knocking noise, while others swore it was the sound of deep laughter. Whatever they thought they heard, the party found the vault empty. On 8 July 1999, Hannah de Wolfe from Holland complained of becoming 'suddenly very cold' in the vault. A few seconds later she hit the ground. Ben Scott couldn't believe his luck. Two days later, 12-year-old Charles Band from Pittsburgh told his mother that something was touching his hair in the Black Mausoleum. In the streetlight, after the tour, his mother found three blood-filled gouges on the child's forehead. On 20 July, Elaine Weyman insisted that something was brushing her face in the vault. Outside the Black Mausoleum, the horrified tour party pointed out to Kate the cut down the back of Elaine's neck. On 15 August 1999, a thumping began at the back of the Black Mausoleum, the temperature dipped and the tomb became so cold that several nervous visitors asked to leave. Ben led them out, protesting that he hadn't finished his story. Five days later Siobhan Reuse from Australia complained of feeling very cold just inside the Black Mausoleum. She tried to push her way out of the vault and collapsed in the doorway. Two days later a tour party, once again, heard thumping noises coming from inside the tomb as they approached. Again, the tomb was empty.

On 1 September 1999, Elizabeth Williams from London felt something she couldn't see touching her face in the Black Mausoleum. The next day she called to say that she had woken up with bruises around her eyes.

Ben Scott sat in Greyfriars pub with Kate. They had just hired a third tour guide, Derek, and were celebrating impending global domination.

'We should celebrate in style,' Ben said as he went up to the bar. 'How about a malt whisky with lime and blackcurrant?'

'I'll stick to lager. You can put a slice of pineapple in it.'

Ben brought the round of drinks back to the table and though they exchanged pleasantries for a while, both knew where the conversation was going. It was Kate who began.

'More and more weird things are happening to people on our tours.'

Ben grinned.

'Great, huh? Maybe we should get some first-aid training.'

'I've already called and made inquiries about it.' Kate looked at Ben over the rim of her glass.

'Well done.'

'It's all a bit odd, love, you have to admit.'

Ben shrugged. 'People get nervous in that tomb. It's all psychosomatic, you know.'

'What about the scratches?'

'That's what children are like. A kid gets scared, he grabs hold of some part of himself and digs in his nails.'

'Really? What part of yourself do you grab when you're scared?'

Ben sipped his pint. 'You know what I mean. The kid puts his hand up to his face, doesn't even realise he's scratched himself.'

'Ben. We've had adults getting scratched as well.'

'Adults are just big kids.'

'What about the cold spots?'

'Draughts.'

'Thumping noises?'

'Minor earthquakes.' Ben scratched his chin. 'I don't know. It doesn't matter, does it?'

Kate took out a tobacco tin and cigarette papers, placed them on the table and began to roll a cigarette. 'C'mon, you're the one who's been reading up on all sorts of daft poltergeist theories. Have you ever read about a spook that's as helpful as ours?'

'Sort of. Ever heard of a ghost called Philip?'

'No. Who was he?'

'Nobody.'

And Ben Scott told Kate the story of the ghost that haunted itself.

In the 1970s, eight members of a Canadian group called the Toronto Society for Psychical Research embarked on an experiment. Though they had often claimed to have held successful séances, their aim was to prove that paranormal phenomena were nothing to do with the 'spirit world'. The group believed that, given the right circumstances, so-called 'spirits' might actually be the subconscious creations of living humans. To illustrate their point, they decided to try and create a ghost called Philip.

The group's scientific adviser, Dr A.R.G. Owen of the University of Toronto, stressed the artificial way in which this ghost was to be characterized: 'It was essential to their purpose that Philip be a totally fictitious character. Not merely a figment of the imagination but clearly and obviously so, with a biography full of historical errors.' So the team came up with a fictional character and began to concoct a life for him. They made Philip a seventeenth-century aristocratic Englishman, a Catholic and a supporter of King Charles I. He lived in Diddingstone Hall, was married to a cold, remote wife called Dorothea and was having an affair with a gypsy girl named Margo. The Society for Psychical Research were obviously better versed in Mills and Boon novels than they were in Cromwellian history. Philip's life story was carefully plotted. Dorothea accused Margo of witchcraft, Margo was executed and Philip, afraid to jeopardise his privileged position, did nothing to prevent it. Later, in a fit of remorse, the unfortunate character killed himself.

Though the Toronto group had no illusions about how unreal Philip was – especially with a plotline like that – they went on to flesh out this imaginary cavalier with more and more intimate details. They acquired photographs of a real Diddingstone Hall in England, which they pretended was Philip's ancestral home. They drew pictures of him, picked his favourite foods, analysed his relationships with Margo and

Dorothea. They obviously had a lot of time on their hands.

What they achieved in the end was a uniform and detailed mental picture of this man. Even though he didn't exist, they all felt they knew him. The term they used was 'collective hallucination'.

Then the group conducted séances and used ouija boards to try and conjure Philip up. Astonishingly, it seemed to work: 'Philip' would answer questions from the group by rapping on their table. He answered their questions, showed likes and dislikes, had strong opinions on some subjects and was hesitant about others. As Iris Own, co-author of the book *Conjuring Up Philip*, put it: 'We clearly understand and have proved that there is no 'spirit' behind these communications; the messages are from the group subconscious, but it is the physical force we need to know more about.' If the experiments were to be believed, a group of eight people had managed to make their collective consciousness form an unexplained physical entity – an entity that had developed rudimentary self-awareness and was able to interact with them.

Kate thought for a while then lit her cigarette. 'What a lot of guff.'

'Aye,' Ben agreed, 'it is.'

He took her lighter and lit a cigarette of his own. A curl of grey smoke drifted up through the jukebox music and blended with the haze already floating above their heads. Kate tapped her cigarette and a few sparks drifted into Ben's pint.

'So you don't think we're doing something like that?'

'Of course not. It's just people's imaginations running away with them.'

'Just as well, eh, love?'

'Why's that?'

'Well, this Philip wasn't too bad a guy – apart from being rotten to women. You'd probably have got on well.'

'Thanks.'

'I mean, these people in Toronto wouldn't try and create something they'd be afraid of, would they?' She blew a ring of smoke and it hung in the air between them. 'But Mackenzie's different, eh?'

Ben saw what Kate was getting at. 'Aye. People on the tour believe in this thing, no doubt about it, and there's a lot more than eight of them.'

'But they think it's evil. If group consciousness ever brings the Mackenzie Poltergeist to life, the group's not going to be thinking about some poncy nobleman. They'll be picturing a monster that lives in a tomb.'

'Wouldn't that be nice,' Ben grinned, sipping his pint again.

Kate arched an eyebrow, a movement Ben found cute and intimidating in equal measure. 'No, Ben. It wouldn't. Not when I go in there every night.' Then she smiled mischievously 'It's quite good, though, eh?'

'Oh yeah.'

Ben grinned and raised his glass. Kate clinked hers against it.

'Aye, love. We certainly know how to scare people.'

At that point, neither Ben nor Kate considered the notion that the terror visitors felt in the Black Mausoleum might not actually be due to them.

Charity

Charity Pirkle entered the Covenanters' Prison on 29 July 2000:

> I have been to Edinburgh only once in my life and, when I told a friend of mine I was visiting, she mentioned a 'City of the Dead Tour' she had gone on when she was there. It sounded interesting, so I went one Saturday night with my friend Adrian. She's from Birmingham, Alabama, and I'm from Atlanta, Georgia. We were both 17 at the time. This was sometime in July 2000.
>
> When we started out, we were both realistic about the evening – expecting to learn some history and hear some scary stories. The tour went, we assume, as normal until we got to the Covenanters' Prison. We all had to promise that City of the Dead was not responsible for anything that happened while we were inside, and Adrian and I got a little nervous at that. But that was why we were there, to be frightened, in a fun way. Neither of us thought that there would actually be an encounter with the Mackenzie Poltergeist.
>
> When we walked into the Covenanters' Prison we were kind of quiet, just looking around at the area that we had come into. I was facing Adrian, about to ask her a question, when I felt something poke me hard in my left side. I thought that I had accidentally backed into someone, but when I turned to apologise, there wasn't anyone there! Puzzled, I nevertheless passed it off as a trick of the mind and continued walking towards the Black Mausoleum.

I didn't want to miss any part of the tour so Adrian and I were the first in and stood toward the back of the small dark room. As our tour guide told us about the different things that had gone on in the area, Adrian and I could hear an echo coming from the back of the wall. But when he stopped speaking, I realised that the noise behind me was continuing! It seemed to be coming from the wall at about head height and continued on and off while the guide was speaking.

Adrian and I looked at each other, but right at the back and up against the wall, we seemed to be the only ones who could hear the sound. By the time we left the tomb I was scared half to death but still trying to act calm – in fact, I was the last one out of the mausoleum. Then, as I was coming out, something grabbed my right ankle – it felt like a man's hand in a thick glove or wrapped in something very soft.

Half an hour later my ankle had a bruise running all the way round it.

Poltergeist!

Temperament, disposition, talent, environment, heredity. . .
all or any of these may be involved. Some people have
short tempers, others the patience of a saint. Some people
work off their tensions, confusions or rage by playing
squash, listening to old Gong albums, drinking whisky, or
even robbing banks. Some become comedians.
    Some produce poltergeists.
REUBEN STONE, *ENCYCLOPAEDIA OF THE ENEXPLAINED*

What exactly is a poltergeist? Everyone is familiar with the
term, which is a combination of the German words *poltern* 'to
knock', and *geist*, 'spirit'; in other words, a 'noisy spirit'.
According to folklore, poltergeists are mischievous, and
occasionally malevolent, entities that play tricks on their chosen
victims and generally behave in an antisocial way. Often drops
in temperature, rapping noises and unpleasant smells accompany
their presence

Whatever poltergeists might be, their talents are pretty
limited – they seem designed for the specific purpose of being
as annoying as possible, rather like having a little brother you
can't see. Poltergeists can apparently start fires, throw or hide
small objects, speak in disembodied voices and levitate things. In
more severe cases, the poltergeist may shift large items of
furniture and make things appear from nowhere. They seem to
have happily adapted to the development of technology, causing
interference in telephones and electronic equipment and
turning lights and household appliances on and off. But
poltergeists can have a more sinister aspect. In some cases they
pinch, bite, hit, cut and even sexually attack the living.

In general poltergeist activity starts and stops abruptly and has a life span varying from hours to months, though a few of the cases reported have lasted for years. In almost 60 per cent of the cases recorded in the last two centuries, poltergeist activity took place only at night.

There are four popular explanations of what poltergeist activity might be. Those of a religious persuasion believe it is caused by an unclean spirit or a demon that has entered a victim. The poltergeist is vanquished by exorcism and, contrary to popular religious reports, exorcisms and prayer meetings to cast out unwanted demons are still commonplace in Europe and the USA. According to the church this 'spirit' activity is caused by so-called occult practices like ouija boards or séances, which allow a gateway for demonic entry. This explanation is losing power as civilisation takes Christianity and its doctrines less literally – the only demons that plague people these days are personal ones. But, as we shall see, 'personal demons' may well be the best modern explanation for poltergeist activity.

The second explanation for poltergeists is the spiritual one – the belief that the activity is caused by the spirit of a deceased person that has not moved on to the next plane of existence. According to spiritualists, a poltergeist is just a particularly physical ghost. It gets mad because it isn't where it's meant to be, or because it can't come to terms with a particularly violent or sudden death, which is fair enough, really. In these cases, mediums are used to persuade the spirits to move on or simply to leave their victims alone. Though the spiritual and Christian explanations may sound theologically similar, Christian doctrine firmly specifies that communing with the dead or spirits is not divine and is therefore the work of the devil. Christianity strictly forbids ouija boards, séances and clairvoyancy, which are widely used in the Spiritual movement. Spiritualists are rather more tolerant of their differences with Christians and will seek an exorcism if they think a poltergeist case is more than they can handle.

The third explanation for poltergeists is the obvious one, and the most plausible in many cases. Some poltergeists are simply frauds. Scientific data is notoriously scarce, with a noticeable lack of photographic, electronic or audio evidence, and sensational cases such as the Amityville Horror and the Smurl Poltergeist were soon found to be engineered. Other cases, like the famous 'Enfield Poltergeist' which terrorised the Harper family in 1970s London, seemed to start as a genuine infestation which turned more and more fraudulent as the participants grew to like the media attention.

The final explanation is the scientific one; the belief that poltergeist activity is caused by an as yet unexplained mechanism of the human mind. This is commonly referred to as psychokinesis (PK), a theory that is gradually receiving more respect from mainstream science. After rigorous testing using accepted scientific methods, respected psychologists Hans and Michael Eysenk went as far as to state that they are certain PK exists.

Regardless of which explanation you prefer, poltergeists demonstrate a certain pattern of activity that is repeated, with variations, in almost all cases. Poltergeists usually have a 'focus' and their paranormal activity revolves around certain types of people. Females under the age of 20 are often triggers, as are women going through the menopause, but the focus does not have to be female. In the 1930s the psychologist Nandor Fodor advanced the theory that poltergeist disturbances were caused by humans suffering from intense repressed anger, hostility or sexual tension, regardless of their age or sex. In 1980 a poltergeist plagued a family in Somerset, England and, since the family included two teenage children, it was assumed that they were somehow the cause. In fact, it turned out to be the 49-year-old father who was the focus. Under severe pressure at work, he was suffering from depression and had become impotent. When he received medical attention for his condition the poltergeist vanished.

William Roll, project director of the Psychical Research Foundation in Durham, North Carolina pursued this theory. Starting in the 1960s, Roll studied 116 written reports of poltergeist cases spanning over four centuries in more than 100 countries. Roll's conclusion was that these paranormal activities were the result of 'recurrent spontaneous psychokinesis' (RSPK); spontaneous and unexplained physical effects, often caused by a child or teenager as a way of expressing hostility without the fear of punishment. The individual was not aware of having these abilities or being the cause of such disturbances but was secretly pleased when they occurred. Other investigators have listed a catalogue of malaise associated with affected buildings or families. Poor mental and/or physical health, unresolved emotional tensions, anxiety reactions, sleepwalking, phobias, mania, obsessions, dissociative reactions and schizophrenia are all cited and in some cases therapy or medical treatment eliminated the poltergeist activity. Professor A.R.G. Owen has suggested that 'poltergeistry' is a conversion neurosis – the ability of certain people to convert acute anxiety into noise and the movement of objects.

An example of this is the fact that poltergeist activity in Britain frequently occurs in council houses when a new family has recently moved in. It's easy to imagine that the trauma of such an upheaval, especially to a child who has no say in the matter, might contribute to a burst of poltergeist activity. Then again, it's just as plausible that families could fake poltergeist activity to get rehoused in a better neighbourhood.

If poltergeists really are the product of subconscious resentment in a family member, it may explain why the poltergeist frightens or annoys other family members, yet rarely hurts them. Typical poltergeist activity seems more attention-seeking than malicious. If a poltergeist were actually to injure someone, the family might permanently vacate the building, taking away the attention that the activity seems to demand.

It would seem, however, that poltergeist activity can take place when there is no apparent human focus, or the focus is no longer present. In 1995, the Manchester Anomalous Phenomena Investigation Team investigated a poltergeist case in Rochdale, UK, where paranormal activity continued to take place even though the adolescent who seemed to be the focus and her family were removed from the premises. In 1973 it was demonstrated that a compass needle deflected by a female poltergeist victim continued to oscillate in the area where the force had been generated, even though the woman had gone. The most popular explanation for these phenomena is that psychokinetic power is triggered by psychological conditions, after which its existence is independent of the person who generated it. Traditionalists take this to mean that these people are somehow a channel for a greater force, be it demons, spirits from the great beyond or just some blind cosmic force.

Physical attack is the most sinister feature of the poltergeist. A Romanian peasant girl named Eleanora Zugen was afflicted by marks on her body whenever her particular 'poltergeist' was insulted and, at the slightest provocation, scratches and bite marks would appear on the girl's face and arms. In 1980 a physicist named Dr Fleur investigated a poltergeist afflicting a family in Mulhouse, France. This poltergeist was different from typical cases in several ways: to begin with, it had already been active for three years and, rather than just being mischievous, it had become openly hostile to its own focus. Activity seemed to centre round the wife, Carla, who claimed the entity would punch her in the stomach and pinch her legs, which would then become bruised. She also developed mysterious cuts and scratches, would feel 'cold hands' on her neck (which left marks the next day) and the house was subject to sudden massive fluctuations in temperature. When their young son began to talk in his sleep and tell the investigators about 'visitors' that nobody else could see, the family sold the house and moved to the Antilles, on the other side of the world.

At first, the Mackenzie Poltergeist seemed like a standard paranormal case, displaying some typical poltergeist activities, though not all of them. There was no rapping, only a few bangs, and no movement of household objects – hardly surprising since the poltergeist wasn't in a house. There was nothing near the tomb, in fact, for it to move. When the activity spread to surrounding houses, however, banging and movement of objects did begin. Cold spots were frequent – no small feat on a winter's night in Scotland – victims would complain of suddenly feeling 'freezing cold' inside. Cuts and bruises and the sensation of being touched or grabbed were also regular occurrences. But there were major differences between the Mackenzie case and other poltergeists. Since different people entered the Covenanters' Prison each night, it followed that the Mackenzie poltergeist couldn't possibly have one person as a focus. If there was a focus it would have to be the guide, since the guides were the only people who entered the area every night. Spiritualists had no problem justifying their explanation. Unlike a house, the graveyard, with its terrible history, could be the site of countless restless spirits.

There was another, still more significant difference between the Mackenzie Poltergeist and other recorded cases. Every night, inside the Black Mausoleum, the tour guides deliberately brought about conditions of stress in the parties they conducted. In the blackness of a graveyard tomb – famous for having an active poltergeist – visitors listened to the guide describe exactly what this thing could do. Suddenly it was no longer a game and a whole rash of negative emotions could be elicited – emotional tension, severe anxiety, phobic or manic reaction, terror, hostility and resentment – in many cases repressed by individuals trying not to show their fear in front of friends, relatives or partners. These were optimum conditions for the creation of poltergeist activity; if you subjected a wide range of people to the same negative emotions night after night you had a scenario never seen in a paranormal case before. The Mackenzie Poltergeist may have evolved not as an entity with no human focus – but as the first case of a poltergeist with dozens of them. Enough to leave a psychokinetic residue in the tomb it inhabited – a residue that was added to by focus after focus and fed, night after night, by negative emotions.

If this were true, Mackenzie would have a freedom that other poltergeists did not enjoy. As the product of dozens of negative minds, rather than one, surrounded by strangers rather than family, it was free to attack anyone at all. Not just to pinch and scratch them, but to knock them out.

To put it in religious terms, the Mackenzie Poltergeist was legion.

At its epicentre, in the Black Mausoleum, the entity wasn't interested in rapping out messages or moving small objects. It was a different kind of creature entirely. Time and time again, visitors insisted on leaving the tomb before their tour had finished, convinced they could feel the poltergeist's presence. The impression it gave them was not that of a mischievous trickster who simply wanted to frighten.

It was that of a predator stalking its prey.

Gail

Statement given by Gail Baird. Gail lived for six months in one of the flats overlooking Greyfriars graveyard before moving in with her future husband.

John, the man I was seeing (and who is now my husband), used to poke fun at me when he came to visit, because I'd regale him with more and more unexplained goings-on in my flat. He is one of life's confirmed sceptics and his being an astrophysics student at the time didn't help. I imagine every scientist wants absolute proof of things before committing themselves. (I'm still convinced he only accepted I'd been pregnant when he changed his first nappy.)

Unexplained things happened periodically. I would leave objects in the living-room and they would reappear in the kitchen. The shower room door (which I like to keep shut, obviously) kept opening by itself. Clocks changed their times or broke. But two particular incidents completely freaked me out and made my scientifically minded husband-to-be consider the possibility that there are things that science doesn't have an explanation for. One afternoon John arrived to see me and I was in a terrible state. I had a large collection of soft toys at the time, which I kept in a pile in the corner, on the floor. At about half past twelve I went shopping and, when I got back an hour later, my entire collection of fluffy animals had been piled in a pyramid on the bed. My heart leapt into my throat when I walked into my bedroom and saw it and I shook all day. John was convinced that I had put them there in a fit of tidying and forgotten about it. I don't call piling animals in geometric shapes tidying up, and there is nothing wrong with my memory.

The second incident even John couldn't explain. We arrived back from a night out at about 2.30 in the morning. It had been a good night and although we were not drunk, we were pretty giggly. However, the living-room sobered us up rather quickly. Every one of the pictures that had been hanging on the walls were now on the floor. But they hadn't fallen. At least, if they had fallen, they had managed to land in a neat pile in the middle of the carpet. We couldn't think of anything else to do, so we rehung them and went to sleep.

Uneasily.

The Inductor

induct-ance: (-*ans*) n. The property of an electric circuit by which a varying current in it produces a magnetic field that induces voltages in the same or nearby circuit.
induct-ee: *n.* A person inducted.

OXFORD ENGLISH DICTIONARY

Typical of these incidents was a college lecturer's claim to feel a hand pressed over her mouth as she walked through the Covenanters' Prison. She fainted and when she came round she noticed a strange mark on her cheek and neck. She remains convinced the bruises were not the result of the fall.

'Edinburgh's Ghoulden Years',
EDINBURGH EVENING NEWS, 20 OCTOBER 2000

Ben Scott was about to give his usual warning. For over an hour he had herded his walking tour party – numbering around 25 – through the high-sided wynds of the Royal Mile then over the silent headstone-studded hillocks of Greyfriars graveyard. After three months of taking City of the Dead tours he had achieved the balance he wanted between facts and entertainment and each dark historical tale was now laced with equally black humour.

The wynds at night were sinister and claustrophobic but it wasn't until they entered the silent graveyard that the tour party's laughs became tinged with nervousness. The moon was full and it radiated a sickly light that turned the shadows moating each ancient tomb into midnight pools. In the centre of the graveyard, the crouching, compact hulk of Greyfriars church cast the deepest, blackest shadow of all. The visitors looked around anxiously and shuffled nearer to the lucky couple who had been given flashlights. A chill breeze had sprung up and autumn leaves spiralled out of the starless night, brushing the faces of unsuspecting listeners and eliciting terrified squeaks or manly shudders.

Now the party stood outside the gates of the Covenanters' Prison. To the left loomed the ribbed dome of Bluidy Mackenzie's tomb, and to the right was the slightly less impressive Georgian mausoleum housing the mortal remains of the architect James Adams. Across the gate itself a thick chain gleamed in the moonlight, fastened by an impressively large padlock.

Ben dangled the key from his gloved hand.

'Ready?'

The visitors didn't look ready at all. Ben unlocked the chain with a flourish and the gate creaked slowly open.

'Ladies and gentlemen, welcome to Jurassic Park.'

The visitors laughed uncertainly, wondering whether there really was a monster lurking beyond that barrier. At this moment they were painfully reminded that this was not a movie they could turn off if things went wrong.

'Oh. Before we go in. I forgot something.' The visitors heaved a sigh of relief.

Ben launched into his warning. It was a standard disclaimer and all the tour guides gave a variation of it. He described the ways in which the poltergeist operated and emphasised that if anyone who was asthmatic, pregnant, claustrophobic or had a weak heart insisted on going in, they only had themselves to blame.

Then he threw in the killer line.

'Is anyone here an inductor?'

The visitors looked at each other in puzzlement. *Was* anyone here an inductor? Nobody had a clue. Nobody knew what an inductor was.

Ben raised a dramatic eyebrow, though nobody could actually see it in the darkness. An inductor, he told the audience theatrically, was a type of person who attracted a poltergeist. In fact, sometimes they even *created* one. Strictly speaking, this wasn't true. People who attract or create a poltergeist are called the 'focus', as Ben well knew, but inductor sounded better. Given the dubious origins of the word, it was a safe bet that nobody was going to admit to being one, and this instance was no exception.

Ben led his silent group through the gates. They edged warily down the shadowy canyon of the Covenanters' Prison like a miniature seventh cavalry, gargoyle-laden tombs rising on either side in an uncomfortable reminder that death was, literally, all around. Ben stopped outside the Black Mausoleum and swung back its iron gate. This one was well oiled, so he had to make the creaking noise out of the corner of his mouth. He shone his flashlight into the black gaping maw.

'In you get, folks,' he enthused. 'Me? Oh no. I never go first. Carry on. Right to the back.'

The crowd shuffled reluctantly inside.

'It's really dark back here,' a voice drifted out from the tomb's interior. The crowd paused in a little bottleneck of fear.

'I know,' said Ben sympathetically. 'But the poltergeist likes to attack at the front of the tomb.'

The crowd surged forward again.

'There. Knew you'd all fit.'

Safely last, Ben strolled into the vault. There came a polite cough from outside and he turned in surprise. A tall, burly figure stood silhouetted in the vault doorway. The moonlight spread a silver sheen over his glasses, obscuring his expression.

'C'mon, get in here,' Ben beckoned.

'S'cuse me, sir,' said the straggler, politely but firmly. 'I reckon I'm one of those inductors.'

The accent was unmistakable, from somewhere in the deep south of the United States. Ben, who had lived for several years in America, recognised it as Texan. He sighed. 'Now, what would make you think that?' he inquired, equally politely.

''Cause I been in a place where there was a poltergeist before.'

'Ah.'

'An' it attacked me.'

'Oh.'

There was a hush from the crowd at the back of the tomb. Ben could almost hear knuckles whitening.

'In that case, don't get in here. In fact, get right over there.' He pointed to the graveyard wall opposite. It was about 30 feet away, as far from the Black Mausoleum as the American could go without being out of sight entirely. The Texan was happy to oblige. He trotted over to the wall and leant against it facing the tomb. Ben turned back to his group, searching for a way to turn the situation to his advantage.

'Can you all see him?' he whispered.

The tour party nodded.

'If he really is an inductor, something's going to happen to him. This thing normally takes a while to get going – you know, before it does anything. I usually finish the tour and get out of here before something goes wrong.' He paused to let the implications of the word 'usually' sink in.

'If this gentleman really is an inductor,' Ben continued, '*if* he is, I bet something happens to him straight away. Keep your eyes peeled.'

Some of the more astute visitors unshouldered their cameras. The Texan obligingly lit a cigarette and its tiny red pinpoint cast a demonic glow onto his spectacles. Ben waited. Nothing happened. He hadn't really expected anything but it was worth a try. He turned back to his group. 'All right, ladies and gentleman,' he began. 'Here we are in the Bla . . .'

There was a soft thud to his left, followed by a horrified gasp. One of the tour party lay on the ground. Ben crouched beside the motionless man, signalling the rest of the crowd to stay where they were. The fallen figure was a male in his mid-twenties. Ben recognised him as one of a small group of Norwegians who had joined the tour.

'Sorry,' said the fallen Norwegian in a muffled voice. He lifted himself off the damp soil with a swift push-up and staggered to his feet, shaking his head in surprise. 'It's all right. All right,' he said sheepishly. 'I lose my balance. This is all.'

The group burst into thankful laughter, some of it verging on maniacal. Ben heaved a hammy sigh of relief. 'As I was saying,' he grinned, 'Ladies and gentlemen, here we are in the Bla . . .'

The Norwegian went down again.

'Stay right where you are,' Ben cautioned, crouching down again. 'Everything will be fine.'

This time the Norwegian lay motionless. He seemed to be out cold.

'It's all right. Happens all the time!' But the tension in Ben's voice was obvious. 'He'll be fine. A couple of minutes and he'll be wide awake and right as rain. Honestly. I've seen it all before . . . What the . . .?'

The tour party looked up, eyes wide.

The lone Texan was loping enthusiastically across the grass towards them. Flinging his cigarette into the darkness, he burst into the vault and grabbed the unconscious Norwegian under each arm. 'I got ya, buddy!' he grimaced, and began to drag the unresisting man out of the tomb.

'Oh, for God's sake!' Ben groaned, struggling to his feet. 'Here. You and you, help get him outside. Careful now. Not *everybody*!'

Two able-bodied youths, the Norwegian's friends, moved forward and helped lift their motionless companion. Along with the Texan, they began an awkward six-legged shuffle, disappearing through the tomb door like a giant crab. Ben turned back to the crowd to size up the situation. Tour parties could range from rabidly sceptical to unquestioningly accepting and their attitude greatly affected their behaviour. From experience Ben knew that most men in the group, even if they were genuinely scared, wouldn't show it. The same was true of parents and older women. But the bulk of this tour party was young, female and clearly scared. Up to this point they hadn't really cared whether the stories were true or not, they were happy enough to get carried away by the atmosphere of the tour. But now there was an unconscious Norwegian being carried away instead and the thrill of a ghostly adventure had been replaced by an alarm that bordered on panic. Many were considering the possibility that there really was a malevolent entity in the darkened tomb alongside them.

Ben had done enough sizing up. 'Right,' he said confidently. 'I think it's time we left.' The crowd's relief was palpable. 'I want everyone to make their way towards the doorway. Not all at once! Take your time, stay together, move slowly. There's plenty of time.'

The crowd began to shuffle forward, Ben directing them towards the sanctuary of the open air with the efficiency of a traffic cop, an image enhanced by the amount of black leather he was sporting.

He never did find out who screamed. It came from the back of the party, in the darkest, farthest corner of the Black Mausoleum – a horrified female voice ringing out. 'It's got my head!' the woman shrieked. 'It's in my hair!' Nobody could see what had 'got' the young lady in question. It might have been a prank – one of her friends grabbing her in the blackness. She may have got her hair caught in a crack in the wall as she moved away from it. Maybe something supernatural really did slap her on the head. Whatever caused it, the terror in the woman's voice was all too genuine. The crowd surged forward.

It's a rule of nature that, in the event of danger, flashlights either stop working or turn out to be in the possession of those too petrified to use them. Ben's £30 Maglite was swept from his hand as he tried to hold back 25 shambling bodies and broke as soon as it hit the ground. The other two flashlight holders in the group had been placed on either side of the crowd, at the front of the vault, to shed maximum light. They immediately shot out of the door, leaving everyone else in pitch blackness.

The crowd burst into a terrified run. Ben wisely pressed himself against the tomb wall and let them stream past.

Fear has a wonderful way of disorienting people. Pouring through the vault doorway, the panicked crowd had no idea in which direction to head. The moon had vanished behind a cloud and now it was as dark outside as it had been in the Black Mausoleum. The two flashlight bearers, remembering the *Jurassic Park* joke, had switched their torches off rather than attract the poltergeist's attention by waving a beam of light around. With an instinct for survival that must have originated with cavemen fleeing sabre-tooth tigers, half the crowd intuitively sprinted to the left and half to the right. Those who had gone left soon realised their error, coming to a dead-end after 20 yards. Unwilling to become stationary targets, they trundled around in the darkness yelling for help and looking for the non-existent exit. Those who had gone the right way soon found themselves, to their immense relief, heading for the gates of the Covenanters' Prison, but failed to notice the overhanging branches lurking between them and salvation. Three or four scurried right through them, only to encounter what felt like long, thin fingers brushing over their faces. There was a renewed bout of screaming. One woman turned and ran back the way she had come, shouting that the poltergeist was trying to eat her eyes.

The two Norwegians let go of their rigid companion and stared in disbelief as this human pandemonium emerged from the darkness and surged around them. The Texan gamely carried on, but the sudden jolt of his feet being dropped had brought the comatose Norwegian to his senses. The last thing he remembered was standing in the Black Mausoleum. Now he was being dragged backwards through the graveyard by something he couldn't see. He let loose with a stream of hysterical Norwegian invectives in which the word 'poltergeist' was clearly audible several times and the Texan finally dropped him.

It took almost 15 minutes to get everyone out. One girl was found hiding on the floor of another tomb with her arms over her head. Several people sported impressive cuts and bruises but couldn't tell if they'd been caused by something supernatural or by running into headstones in the dark.

Ben stood by the gates of the Covenanters' Prison trying to get his heart to stop thumping. He had taken his shaken group to the graveyard entrance and bade them farewell. The Norwegian, it seemed, was none the worse for his ordeal. In fact he couldn't remember much of what had happened which, Ben concluded, was probably a good thing. The Texan had introduced himself as Leon Hill, shaken Ben's hand warmly and insisted that he hadn't had such a fine time in years. It turned out he came from Louisiana. Despite their mixed feelings, the rest of the tour party had agreed that it wasn't an outing they were ever likely to forget.

The Norwegians beckoned Ben over. 'We do not wish to be impolite,' one of them said in hushed tones. 'We know you will probably tell others about this . . . incident.'

'That's a fair bet,' Ben admitted.

'We . . . eh . . . we in Norway are not the type to be scared by poltergeists. To . . . *believe* in poltergeists. We certainly do not fall down for no reason.'

'And?'

'We were thinking it would be better if you told people we were Swedish.'

The rest of the tour party was drifting shakily out into the street. Ben turned and indicated in the direction they had just come from. 'I forgot to lock the bloody gate. Anybody want to come and help?'

The tour party looked as if he'd suggested they eat their own livers.

'Didn't think so.'

Ben turned and trudged back into the darkness.

'I'll come with you,' an American teenager in engineer pants and a baseball cap peeled off from the group. 'I wanna take one last look at that place.'

Nodding, two of his friends joined him.

Ben glanced back. 'You coming, Leon?'

'I don't think I will,' grinned the Louisianan. 'Thanks for asking, though.'

Ben and the Americans walked back to the Covenanters' gate and locked it without further incident. They stood gazing through the bars at the peaceful shadowy strip of cemetery. The Americans lit cigarettes. 'So . . . does this kind of thing happen every night?' asked one of the young men.

'If it did I would have quit a long time ago.'

His friend looked thoughtful. 'Do you think it's real?' he asked Ben.

Ben turned away from the gates and shook his head. 'I don't know,' he said.

The Americans nodded. 'Cool.'

With that they turned and headed back towards the real world.

Alan

Alan Vickers is from North Wales. On 5 August 2000 he witnessed the collapse of Deirdre Quirk from Ireland in the Black Mausoleum.

Last year I had the pleasure of experiencing what happens to people in Greyfriars graveyard. Now, I will admit to being slightly sceptical. I live in Edinburgh now, and people from Edinburgh think it's funny that it has such a reputation as a haunted city. I had heard about the Covenanters' Prison and all the things that are supposed to go on there. That's the reason I went on the tour in the first place. I'd never really wanted to go on anything like this before but it sounded like it might be a bit of a laugh.

So, armed with all of this prior knowledge, a friend and myself went along one evening to see exactly what all the fuss was about. I enjoyed the tour, it was funny and informative, but I can't say that I was particularly scared. Then came the part we'd all been warned about, and that I'd been looking forward to. Entering the Covenanters' Prison at the back of Greyfriars cemetery is a very unusual experience. Here you are in the middle of this great city, surrounded by hustle and bustle, yet you have no sense of it once you get inside. There is hardly any noise; the whole area feels still. It was deep into twilight by the time our tour arrived there and were herded along towards the Black Mausoleum.

The tour party was probably about 30 people strong. Some were tourists, some had read articles about the Mackenzie Poltergeist and others were just out to be entertained. Throughout the tour we had been told about the mausoleum and, before entering, people with heart conditions and those of a nervous disposition were asked to wait outside. Whether it was this that caused it, or the surroundings, there was a real sense of unease amongst the group when we were packed into the mausoleum itself. It was cramped, damp, and as dark as I have ever experienced – you could barely see past the outline of the person two feet ahead of you. It was very unsettling and an incredible experience, feeling the unease growing, trapped in this dark place. The group was silent, each member deep in their own little thoughts. All the same, I just could not believe that this feeling was being created by anything but our own paranoia and vivid imaginations.

From the doorway, looking in, I was at the right-hand wall, near the back. Nearer the front, over at the left-hand wall, there was suddenly a heavy thump followed by screaming. A girl was lying on the ground. The quiet atmosphere broke. Panic spread like a wave and people started moving, then muttering, and then people began to shout: 'Let me out,' 'I want to leave,' 'Get out,' as the group fought its way out into the relative safety of the twilight. Once she had been carried out, however, the girl quickly regained consciousness.

As I said, I'm a sceptic and not frightened by stories or dark places, but at the same time, I cannot quite explain or describe the feeling I had in that tomb. Maybe it was just my subconscious picking up on the group's collective unease. All the same, I'm now a much easier man to convince of the possibility of poltergeists. As for my friend, I think she is easier to convince too. Although it was dark and I was uneasy, I was well aware of everything that was going on. I know for a fact that at no time did my friend fall, bump into anything or get pushed by anyone.

Yet the morning after the tour, she had bruises on her body and scratches down her back.

The Exorcist

But as the ceremony drew to a close a shadow glided
across the Greyfriars Kirk's window — although the doors
were locked and no one was inside.

'So what is that figure lurking in a window?'
EDINBURGH EVENING NEWS, 15 NOVEMBER 1999

At the time, Mr Grant said, 'I hoped I had exorcised all the
spirits but it appears one had been hiding.'

'Exorcist minister dies trying to contact dead'
THE EXPRESS, 29 JANUARY 2000

On 25 September 1999, a male visitor on a City of the Dead
tour spotted something white flitting between the tombs in
Greyfriars. It appeared to be following the tour party. Kate
Kavanagh, who was taking the tour, did not see anything and
suggested it might be a fox or even a child playing a prank, but
the gentleman found the sight distressing enough to leave the
group and graveyard immediately. After that the tour resembled
a wagon train. Those at the back looked nervously behind and
the whole party seemed ready to form a defensive circle at a
moment's notice.

Two days later, Ben Scott was in full storytelling flow when
an Australian male in his mid-twenties plunged to the floor of
the Black Mausoleum. The unconscious antipodean woke up
five minutes later, profoundly embarrassed and declining to give
his name, though he did insist that he had never fainted before
in his life. Young Australian males, apparently, didn't do that kind
of thing.

On 10 October several of Kate's party again saw 'something white' moving between the graves. Again, this unidentified stalker seemed to unduly frighten those members who spotted it, and three of them left the graveyard. Kate stared after them in consternation. 'Am I missing something here?' she demanded of the agitated group.

On 13 October an English visitor was overcome with nausea in the Black Mausoleum. Swaying slightly, she reached out to the woman next to her for support. As her hand touched the stranger's shoulder the second woman looked at Ben Scott with sudden panic. 'My legs are frozen,' she said in an astonished voice, then proved herself partially wrong by taking several steps forward before collapsing in the doorway.

The Mackenzie Poltergeist had come to the attention of the press by this time and local newspapers invited a well-known spiritualist minister, the Reverend Colin Grant, to come and give his opinion of the graveyard disturbances. Ben Scott was also invited.

A small, strange-looking group gathered in the graveyard on a chilly afternoon in November – Ben Scott, Colin Grant and his wife, a reporter named Claire Gardner and a press photographer. Colin Grant, a stout, friendly man with a down-to-earth manner, shook Ben's hand and asked where the trouble seemed to be. Ben hadn't really thought of the poltergeist as trouble before, but it occurred to him that Colin Grant saw this as a rescue mission rather than a publicity stunt. 'Come with me,' Ben said.

The photographer had wandered off to take shots of the most impressive tombs and Mrs Grant had wisely opted to stay in the car, so only Claire and Colin accompanied their guide to the Covenanters' Prison.

Colin Grant didn't talk much. Instead, he looked around as he walked in a manner that implied he was taking in more than just the sights. The sky was grey and overcast and a strong biting wind tore through the leafless branches above his head. Claire Gardner chatted animatedly to Ben and Colin as they neared the gates of the Covenanters' Prison, remarking several times how creepy the graveyard seemed and how it gave her the shivers. As far as Ben could see, temperatures like this would give a penguin the shivers, but he assumed it was a journalistic trick to put them all in the right frame of mind. Ben never saw the graveyard as creepy during daylight hours – the worst it could manage was an austere, lonely beauty. On this gusting, granite day Greyfriars merely seemed hostile, coldly poking at the little group with sharp windy fingers.

Ben reached the Covenanters' Prison ahead of the others, unfastened the padlock and threw open the gate. The wind howled up the line of tombs and shuffled a herd of dying leaves across the scrubby grass. A sudden blast swept grit into Ben's face. He stepped back, rubbing at his eyes, to let Colin Grant go through. Colin had stopped uneasily in the gateway. 'We don't have to go in if you don't want to,' said Claire Gardner sympathetically, though Ben failed to see how she'd have a story unless they did. Colin simply nodded, took a deep breath, and walked through the gates.

As soon as he entered he staggered sideways, almost overbalancing, and clung shakily to one of the tomb walls. It looked as if a particularly strong surge of wind had hit the minister. Claire and Ben looked at each other in genuine surprise. Colin Grant was muttering to himself and seemed disoriented and in pain. Clutching at his head he straightened up, let go of the wall, and slowly and carefully backed out of the Covenanters' Prison.

Ben locked the gate while Claire helped Colin to a nearby grass verge. The minister sat down heavily, his face pallid and grey and his breathing laboured. He looked up as Ben approached. 'There are many spirits in pain through there,' he said matter-of-factly. 'Many.' Then he looked directly at Ben and beckoned him closer. 'There is something else as well. Something much stronger.'

At the urging of the same newspaper, Colin Grant went back to Greyfriars on 14 November 1999. Convinced that hundreds of spirits had become somehow trapped in the Covenanters' Prison, he agreed to exorcise the area. Again he was accompanied by Claire Gardner and her photographer. This time, Ben didn't bother to go.

Armed with a bible and 14 candles, Grant entered the prison and made his way to the centre of the area. He laid out 12 candles in a circle with another two behind and placed two small crosses in the ground for protection. The wind was blowing hard once again. He had trouble lighting the candles, but the witnesses swore that once they were lit the flames stood erect, as if the wind no longer had the power to affect them. Colin Grant let the bible fall open and began to recite.

There was no wailing or roaring or gnashing of teeth. Nobody vomited green slime. The journalist's and photographer's heads did not spin round. After ten minutes the Reverend Colin Grant walked out of the Covenanters' Prison and told those watching that the trapped spirits had been freed. He looked exhausted and physically ill and as he once again lowered himself onto the grass verge, he made a macabre remark: 'This has taken a lot out of me,' he said, matter-of-factly. 'It'll most probably kill me.'

The reporters assumed he was joking.

Neither Claire Gardner nor Ben Scott realised how deeply troubled Colin Grant was by what he had encountered – he confided to his son, Colin junior, that Greyfriars was like 'nothing else I've experienced'. According to the Reverend Grant, he had 'freed' at least 200 spirits from an indescribable sense of woe, but he also repeated that there were 'bigger and stranger' forces in the Covenanters' Prison that had not yet been removed. Colin Grant fully intended to go back and face whatever had unnerved him so much in that patch of graveyard. But first he needed to recover from the struggle he had just endured, one he felt had mentally and physically exhausted him.

He never did.

The Reverend Colin Grant collapsed and died on 21 January 2000.

If Colin Grant was right about freeing hundreds of trapped spirits from the Covenanters' Prison, he was also right, it seemed, about leaving something behind. The night after the exorcism Lorena Ramirez from Mexico began to choke as soon as she entered the Black Mausoleum. Gasping that something was 'pressing on her throat', she dashed from the vault. As she ran she scattered Colin Grant's candles, still set in a circle on the grass outside.

The next month, a college lecturer named Sharon Brewster was standing in the Black Mausoleum when she felt a sensation 'like hands holding her throat'. She tried to get out of the vault but collapsed in the doorway. When she woke up next day she had a friend take photographs of her face. All down one side, and around her neck, were vivid yellow bruises, as if she had been physically assaulted – as if something powerful had held her by the throat and hit her.

The Mackenzie Poltergeist seemed to have become stronger than ever.

Kate

Statement by Kate Kavanagh, tour guide and director of City of the Dead.

Ben Scott and myself established the City of the Dead tour in 1998 and I have worked as a guide on the tours from the very beginning. Although I enjoy my job, from time to time I sense something in the Covenanters' Prison I cannot explain.

On occasion, when I take the tour party through the gates and into the prison, a feeling of fear overcomes me. It is as though something alive is with us in the darkness, lurking in the shadowy tombs. I cannot say if this is my imagination or if it is the fear and uneasiness of the tour party that I am picking up on, or if something really is in there, waiting, and making its presence known. During the past two years I have had many people on my tours requesting, or rather demanding, to leave the mausoleum, as they too seem to have felt this strange presence. Some are even more sensitive and will refuse to enter the mausoleum, preferring to listen to the tour from the safety of the doorway.

The night of 16 September 2000 is a good example of the type of thing that happens. The tour had been going well and all its members had been enjoying tales of Old Edinburgh. They had cringed in horror when I told them about the atrocities committed at the North Berwick witch trials, sniggered at the true story of Greyfriars Bobby and shuddered at the tales about Edinburgh's infamous bodysnatchers. As I said, all seemed well. Then it was time to go to the back of the graveyard and enter the Covenanters' Prison.

We gathered in the darkness at the padlocked gates and I began to tell them a little about poltergeists, and about this poltergeist in particular. It was at this point that the group realised the tour was getting a lot more sinister and a few visitors were beginning to feel uneasy. I turned to unlock the padlock and unchain the old metal gates, when I too felt a sense of something I had not been aware of in other parts of the graveyard. It hit me very quickly and I didn't understand what I was feeling. I took a deep breath. I didn't want the tour party to know that I was suddenly genuinely scared; for the guide to be as terrified as the customer isn't very professional.

I unlocked the padlock, removed the chain and slowly pushed the gate open. I stepped inside and swiftly encouraged the rest of the tour party to follow me. I suddenly felt I wanted to stay close to them and didn't stride ahead as usual. 'Stay close. There's safety in numbers,' I assured them. But I was really reassuring myself. As we walked down the Covenanters' Prison, towards the Black Mausoleum, I could hear myself breathing faster and my heart was far too fast. Something was not right. I couldn't say what, and I still can't, but I had never felt like this before. We entered the Black Mausoleum, the tour party slowly shuffling forward in a protective huddle. I paused. I was not going to let my imagination get the better of me. Nothing had ever happened to me before, why would it now?

I started speaking with new confidence. I had decided that everything would be fine. It was getting near to the end of the tour. Nothing had happened. I laughed inside at how stupid I had been. I didn't feel afraid any more. If there really had been something in the prison, it had moved somewhere else.

Suddenly I heard a scream, followed by a thud. I

turned on my torch and, as the tomb lit up, the rest of the tour party also screamed and surged backwards, flattening themselves against the wall. A girl lay face down on the floor.

Panic struck. The girl's boyfriend began trying to lift and revive her and I ran over and checked that she was breathing. Having received emergency medical training I was reluctant to move her but, all of a sudden, I had the same feeling as I had earlier. As if something malevolent had materialised right beside me and beside the fallen girl. Suddenly I felt real terror, as if it was about to attack us in the darkness. The two nearest members of the tour party grabbed the unconscious girl, as if they felt the same thing – and the four of us carried her outside.

The rest of the tour party quickly followed. As we waited for the girl to begin to recover properly the group became even more eager to leave the prison. They had felt what I felt and certainly didn't want to hang around to see if the Mackenzie Poltergeist was going to give a repeat performance.

I knelt down. 'What's your name?' I asked the girl.

'Lucy McDade,' she replied.

'Can you stand up?' I asked.

She nodded. Her boyfriend helped her up and we all began our walk back to the gates of the Covenanters' Prison. They seemed very far away. After only a few steps Lucy's legs gave way, her head lolled and she fell back to the ground. 'I'll stay with her,' her boyfriend bravely volunteered. 'You take the rest.' Decisive bloke. Everybody was happy about the idea, including me. We walked quickly to the cemetery gates and I said goodbye, then ran back to the Covenanters' Prison, keeping away from any gravestones that might have something hiding behind them. Lucy had recovered enough to make it out of the prison and I shut and chained the gate.

Afterwards, Lucy swore that she had felt an overwhelming presence closing in around her in the Black Mausoleum. She felt cold and nauseous, and suddenly found it hard to breathe, as if something had cut off her air. The next thing she remembered was opening her eyes to find herself lying on the grass outside the Black Mausoleum. She said she had never fainted before and had never experienced anything like the events that had happened to her on the tour. Though Lucy seemed to relax slightly as we left the cemetery, she turned to her boyfriend and said, 'I will never go in there again.'

I can't say I blame her. I'd been in there a million times – it's a scary place, but this night was different. I think I really felt, for the first time, what the victims of the poltergeist's attacks feel. I always hoped that if it was real, I wasn't its type. I like to think it just made a mistake.

Psychic Tendencies

Spiteful ghosts appear to have returned to Edinburgh's most haunted graveyard, despite the efforts of a spiritualist minister to exorcise them. One of the most recent victims fainted after feeling she was being suffocated and woke up with bruising round her neck.

And just days later, a Californian tourist collapsed after visiting the Covenanters' Prison in Greyfriars Churchyard.

'Back . . . with a vengeance',
EDINBURGH EVENING NEWS, 6 JANUARY 2000

It is Sunday morning and Ms Sneddon is standing in the last tomb in the Covenanters' Prison in Greyfriars Kirkyard, Edinburgh. She has sensed some change in the atmosphere and the dousing crystal she carries everywhere is spinning wildly in an anti-clockwise direction.

Ms Sneddon says, 'There are lots of spirits here and they are not happy . There is a terrible stench of decaying bodies.'

Beside her, the leader of the ghost-hunting expedition, Brian Allen, measures the level of electromagnetic activity. The needle on his meter jerks forward, indicating the presence of something out of the ordinary, but Mr Allen cannot say what it is.

'No rest for wicked in graveyard',
THE *SCOTSMAN*, 6 MARCH 2000

The two mediums stood in the centre of the Covenanters' Prison, each with an arm stretched in front of their body, looking like reluctant superheroes unsure of how to take off. Behind them, Brian Allen and Bill Devlin, heads of the Scottish branch of 'Strange Phenomena Investigators', were sweeping the area with a 'TriField Meter', a machine that looked like a cross between a Geiger counter and a guitar pedal. Near the gates of the Covenanters' Prison an American director and producer, there to film a documentary about the poltergeist, were making notes and talking on their mobile phones. Both were thin and blond and muffled against the March wind, and Ben Scott couldn't tell which was which. He sat on the grass, his back against the Covenanters wall and his feet on a low grave border, dressed in what had now become his trademark black. He was bored.

This was not the first excursion into the Covenanters' Prison for Brian Allen and Billy Devlin. They had already scoured the prison as part of an investigation covered by the *Scotsman* newspaper and BBC Radio Scotland and had claimed, in their written report, to have found evidence of paranormal activity:

> Anne-Marie mentioned that there were spirits moving around us, displeased that we were there. As she said this, the indicator needle abruptly shot fully upscale and dropped immediately back to its former reading. While this may have been a coincidence, I do not believe so – the meter had somehow registered a transient reading, a 'spike' in the local magnetic field.

The SPI and the two mediums had walked the length of the Covenanters' Prison trying to detect supernatural presences. They obviously found the place satisfactorily haunted. According to their report, they spotted a young boy, felt the pain of hundreds of Covenanters and could smell 'death and corruption'. As far as Ben could see, smelling death in a graveyard was like smelling pies in a butcher's shop, but he let it go.

He turned to the two Americans and nodded his head in the direction of the little psychic party investigating their way into the distance. 'So. What's the verdict?'

The producer consulted her notes. 'The mediums say that some sort of bizarre ceremonies have been held here in the past. Possibly witchcraft, but more likely Black Mass and Satanic rituals. They say Edinburgh still has a bunch of practising Wiccan covens.'

'Aye. There are a few around.'

'And that Wiccans can sometimes tip over the edge and turn to devil worship. Ooh. It makes me shiver.'

Ben blew into his hands, white from the nippy spring wind. 'Wicca is a religion based on pre-Christian teachings,' he said. 'Satan is a Christian concept. Wiccans are about as likely to turn to worshipping the devil as they are to worshipping Allah. Besides, what would Satanists be doing in a churchyard?'

'They said this was in the 1800s.'

'You mean when the Old Town was at its most crowded, this place was ringed by tenements full of people and bodysnatchers were getting chased by night watchmen all over the graveyard? Sure. That makes sense.'

The two Americans looked at each other. 'It's only a show.'

'Fine,' said Ben. 'It's just that if there's really something in there, I want it to get fair representation.' And I'm talking like a nutter, he thought to himself.

'Let's go see how they're getting on.' The director pulled her scarf tighter round her throat and marched off down the Covenanters' Prison. The producer helped Ben to his feet. 'Have you ever been attacked?' she asked. 'Ever been hurt?'

'Many times. But never by a poltergeist.'

They walked side by side behind the director.

'You like this thing, don't you?' the producer asked.

'It's invisible. It knocks people down. What's not to like?'

They reached the end of the Covenanters' Prison, where the mediums were revolving slowly, hands outstretched, like large children in some solemn, secret game. Bill motioned the party over and pointed to the TriField meter. 'Look,' he said, pointing excitedly at the flickering needle. 'I'm getting a reading.'

'What does that mean?'

'This measures electromagnetic energy. We think that a lot of paranormal energy may be electromagnetic in origin.' He pointed the meter at the graveyard wall and the needle jumped again.

The Americans consulted their notes. 'What's on the other side of the wall?'

Ben shrugged. 'An electricity generator?'

The investigators scowled at him.

'Joking. Sorry. Actually, I've no idea.'

Bill Devlin scowled too. 'It's funny that we would get a reading way over here, but twice we've had nothing in this Black Mausoleum where all these poltergeist attacks are supposed to have occurred.' Brian pointed the meter at the empty tomb to his right. The needle stayed perfectly still.

The Americans looked at Ben expectantly. Ben blew into his hands again. 'Doesn't surprise me.'

'Why not?'

'That's not the Black Mausoleum.' He pointed. 'It's that one up there.'

The mediums looked sheepish. The Americans glanced at each other and smiled.

The SPI and their psychics did one more investigation, on 6 April 2000, this time accompanied by a BBC film crew. And this time they entered the correct Black Mausoleum. Their second report was very different:

> . . . the rest of the party, eight in number, filed in and stood in silence. The mediums were clearly uneasy. I quickly became aware of feelings of nausea sweeping over me and I felt dizzy, almost as if I was outside my body. Bill glanced at me and leaned against a wall, a grim expression on his face. He told me that he felt very dizzy and squeamish. I left the group in the tomb and went outside into the bright sunshine. The nausea

continued. A few moments later the rest of the group joined me. The mediums looked pale and particularly ill at ease; I did not have to be told that there was something 'not quite right' about the tomb.

As a matter of fact, Ben Scott *had* read up on the theory that electromagnetic energy was behind poltergeist activity. The idea was advanced by the psychic investigator, Albert Budden, who suggested that paranormal phenomena might be the bizarre side-effects of electromagnetic pollution. According to Budden, our landscape is permanently laced with electromagnetic energy, but there are places where this unseen pollution is very dense. These 'hot spots' create powerful standing waves that can actually affect physical laws as well as mental health. Budden claimed that people living in 'hot spots' develop unexpected allergies, nausea, panic attacks, mood swings and, in extreme cases, lapses of consciousness. Though an idea like this would once have been scoffed at, the scientific community now agrees that living under power lines or near powerful transmitters can adversely affect human health. One only has to consider the recent mobile phone/cancer links to see how an apparently harmless piece of technology can be misjudged.

Budden also believed that experiments in electromagnetics by the Canadian scientist, John Hutchison, could explain the physical effects of 'poltergeist activity'. Hutchison crammed a variety of devices such as Tesla coils, Van de Graaff generators and radio frequency transmitters, all of which emit electromagnetic energy, into a single room. He found that after the equipment had been running for a while, effects identical to those commonly regarded as poltergeist phenomena began to occur. Although the electromagnetic energy was low powered, objects hovered in the air or moved about; fires started in the building where Hutchison was working; metal distorted and broke; water spontaneously swirled in containers and lights appeared in the air, then vanished. These phenomena occurred in the same unpredictable way as in reported poltergeist cases. Nothing would happen for days, then coins would flip or water would swirl. The downside of these experiments, of course, was that the electrical apparatus Hutchison was using would then short circuit or malfunction – including, ironically, any monitoring equipment.

Ben Scott and Kate Kavanagh sat in Ben's house drinking wine. It was 11.30 at night; Kate had finished taking a graveyard tour and had stopped in to see him on her way home. Once they had been more than just business partners, and they still had the easy ambience of two people who have known each other well and managed to remain friends.

Ben was being boring. 'Electromagnetic forces, my bum,' he said, pouring himself a large glass. 'It's a graveyard, not a bloody telephone exchange. Of course the needle on that machine flickers. It flickers every time a bloody car goes past.'

Kate came out of the kitchen with another bottle. 'What you getting so het up about? At least they didn't say there was nothing there.'

'I don't want every Joe telepathy and his auntie running through the graveyard spotting the ghost of Little Lord Fauntleroy – we look like idiots for even being on the same planet.'

Kate sat cross-legged on the bed and lit a cigarette. Ben's bed was in his living-room. So was everything else, for that matter. His computer, his books, his guitar, his easel, his CD collection. Ben didn't like to go to too much trouble to get what he wanted. We'll be fine, love.' Kate blew out a stream of smoke. 'All we have to do is tell the truth. We take people into the Black Mausoleum, things happen to them. We don't know why. We can prove they happen – we don't have to explain it.'

'I like explanations.'

'No you don't. You like mystery. You just think that everything *has* to have an explanation.'

'In that case, yes, the graveyard does have an electromagnetic field.'

'Where?'

'Edinburgh University Artificial Intelligence Unit. Where

they try to make machines that think. It backs right against the graveyard wall, ends at the back of the Black Mausoleum, in fact. That place has got to be full of electromagnetic stuff.'

'I suppose so,' Kate agreed.

'And if the Mackenzie Poltergeist isn't an artificial intelligence, I don't know what is.'

'What was that you were saying about not looking like an idiot?'

Ben poured more wine and lit a cigarette. 'I don't know,' he sighed. 'And I don't care anyway. We should talk about something other than business for a change.'

'I like your theory about poltergeists being caused by emotional stress. Hey. Maybe *we* cause it.'

'The two of us? Why? You got any emotional stress?'

'Well, I did.'

It was true. Kate had been in a motorcycle crash in 1995, when another bike had catapulted into her own and almost killed her. She had undergone a long, painful, determined struggle to regain her fiery spirit but, now and again, her old fears rose to the surface. She could lead people through a haunted graveyard at night, but Ben knew Kate was still afraid to cross a road unless the nearest vehicle was a huge distance away.

'Well, *I'm* fine,' Ben said emphatically. 'Being locked in a cupboard as a child and beaten with a cow's tongue in a sock hasn't done me any harm at all.'

He began to twitch one eye convulsively. Kate laughed and poured another glass of wine.

'Yeah, yeah – you don't give a damn about anything and nothing bothers you. Talk about repressed emotions! You've got more emotional baggage than anyone I know.'

'I don't know what you're talking about. I've got an emotional backpack at the very most.'

'Ben. You drink like a fish but you never get drunk. You drive yourself like a slave instead of getting others to help you. You always have a different girl on your arm . . .'

'I have a lot of love to give.'

'. . . so you never have to be alone.'

'Let's talk about business again.' Ben poured another large glass of wine. This time he didn't put lemonade in it. 'Anything happen tonight?'

'Nothing at all, love. Not a thing. Quiet as a grave it was.' Kate raised her glass. 'To Mackenzie. Let's hope he bucks up a bit.'

'To Mackenzie.'

The next week, on Kate's tour, a man – who gave his name only as Mr Richardson – began clutching his head in the Black Mausoleum. Seconds later he pushed his way through the other tour members, staggered towards the vault doorway and collapsed. Kate punched the air in triumph when nobody was looking. The next night a girl named Sharon Ward from South Africa also tried to escape from the tomb, only to collapse in the doorway. She woke again after a couple of minutes and appeared to be none the worse for her experience, which was more than could be said for the rest of the tour party.

Afterwards, Ben decided to relocate to the pub for a stiff drink and several members of the tour party came with him. Halfway through the first round, the pub door opened and Sharon Ward entered. 'Oh. Hi. Do you want a drink? It's on me.' Ben was still concerned that she might be feeling queasy – or in a mood to sue.

Sharon shook her head. 'I was on my way back to the hotel,' she said, 'but my stomach felt all numb. A really weird sensation.' She pulled up her top to show her stomach. 'Look.'

Across her skin were raised weals – just like the marks that would be left by a clawing hand.

Sarah

Statement by Sarah Wilson, a resident of Edinburgh, who entered the Covenanters' Prison in October 2000:

My name is Sarah and I live in Edinburgh. I have done many things, from stand-up comedy to bungee jumping, so I don't scare easily. I have always considered myself to be sceptical when it comes to supernatural events. However, when I went on a tour to Greyfriars with a friend last year, I realised that I may have to look at things in a very different light.

In October 2000, my friend Nicola and I decided to take part in a ghost tour, which seemed like a novel way to spend an evening. We had no preconceived notions of the tour content and we assumed it would be just some actor telling us well-rehearsed stories. The tour party was a fair size, approximately 35 locals and tourists, and we enjoyed the historical content and the humour of the storytelling. When we approached Greyfriars Churchyard we were fairly geared up for the horrors that awaited us in the haunted tombs, though we really didn't expect anything to happen.

My flat is in the Grassmarket, behind Greyfriars, and I used to go there regularly to sketch. I feel I know the graveyard really well and I have never felt or experienced anything strange there, though I had never before been in the part known as the Covenanters' Prison.

However, on the night in question I felt that something was different. As the tour party approached the tomb, we unconsciously began to huddle together.

Edinburgh in October is notoriously cold, but the air as we drew closer to the Covenanters' Prison felt thick and clammy, as if it were stagnant. We were some way back in the group as the guide reached the prison gate and began to unlock it. Standing outside the entrance, the group's fear seemed very strong. Grown men looked nervously in the direction we were heading and no one felt embarrassed, as we all appeared to be feeling the same dread.

Just as the guide motioned to us to move forward, we felt a strange coldness in the atmosphere. It was as if something invisible was moving through the crowd. The temperature had actually dropped, and I could swear it was difficult to breathe. My friend and I even moved to the edge of the group, so odd was the feeling.

Then one lady suddenly fell to the ground as if she had been pushed. We waited for her to get up again, but she just lay there. Looking back, the strangest thing was that no one panicked. It was as if she had been somehow picked out and the rest of us were now safe. I realised I was no longer cold and could breathe properly again. The guide ran over and checked the unconscious woman, who was beginning to show signs of life, but when she tried to stand she could not. Her boyfriend sat down with her, visibly shaken. The woman had regained enough sense to tell us she was all right, but she still could not move and complained that her legs were very cold.

Once he had made sure the woman was comfortable, the guide stood up and asked who was coming with him into the Prison. I could not believe that anyone was actually going to go, but to my amazement everyone followed him, and Nicola and I found ourselves going too! When we talked later we agreed that the realisation there might actually be something supernatural here after all fascinated us so much that we had to find out more. We did not stay in there long however, for the guide was obviously anxious to get back and check that the woman outside was all right. The rest of the tour party did not complain. I got the feeling that they felt the same as me, that if there was something supernatural in the area it was not here but behind us, back at the gate. When we got back the woman was still lying on the ground. She was conscious but still seemed unable to move, and in the end she had to be almost carried to the graveyard exit. The tour party was subdued and nervous and seemed happy to get out.

One thing has stuck in my mind from that night. As the guide walked towards the woman, right after she had fallen down, he passed a few feet from me. I heard him say to himself, 'It's getting stronger.'

There was one other thing I did not notice at the time. When I checked my watch later it had stopped at 9.30 p.m. – the time that the woman had collapsed.

Mute Witness

Colin Grant predicted his confrontation with the spirits of Greyfriars Kirkyard would probably kill him. Some believe it did.

'Did the ghosts of Greyfriars drive Dad to his grave?'
EDINBURGH EVENING NEWS, 5 MAY 2000

I certainly wouldn't rule out a paranormal explanation for what this tour has found.
LIONEL FANTHORPE (HEAD OF THE ASAP), SCOTTISH TELEVISION, MARCH 2000

Colin Grant and the psychic investigations turned out to be only the first wave of attention focused on the Mackenzie Poltergeist. Greyfriars cemetery had featured in local papers regularly since the incidents began and by March 2000 the poltergeist had begun receiving coverage from both national and international media. By this time Kate and Ben were blasé about appearing on television and giving newspaper interviews. The victims of the Mackenzie Poltergeist were not. As more and more media attention focused on them they began, understandably, to clam up. Sharon Brewster found a television crew camped outside her door the day after she gave her first newspaper interview and was harassed by a reporter from the national press when she expressed reluctance to talk to him. She called Ben Scott and told him that she would never discuss the poltergeist, or anything else for that matter, with the press again – a vow she never went back on. Other victims found themselves in similar predicaments. Some became the butt of their friends' jokes. Those with responsible positions couldn't take the chance that media attention of this type would attract criticism at work; there was a big difference in privately believing you had been attacked by a poltergeist and publicly admitting it.

Ben and Kate sat downstairs in the Argyll bar, the pub nearest to Kate's house. Kate lived in Marchmont, a collection of wide, leafy streets lined with Victorian tenements. Each mansion was now divided into dozens of flats and housed a predominantly student population. This suited Kate, who was studying tourism management at university. As far as Ben could see, she had about 800 flatmates.

The Argyll was small, dark and a favoured haunt of students. Perched on a barstool, Ben looked around at the youthful crowd, a mixture of disdain and envy on his face. 'Look at the age of these kids. I'm old enough to be their dad.'

'You're old enough to be *my* dad.' Kate put her hand to her mouth and her eyes widened in wicked glee. 'Sorry, love. Sorry!'

'Only if I had you when I was 12.'

'I wouldn't put it past you. Sorry, love!'

Ben hunched back to his drink. 'You're on the ball today, aren't you?'

Kate nodded cheerfully. 'I am. How come you're looking so fed up?'

Ben sighed and lifted his pint of lager as if the effort of getting it to his lips negated any pleasure he took in drinking it. 'We've got a Polish television company coming in a month to do a documentary about the Mackenzie Poltergeist. Then we've got the US Discovery Channel a few days later. They want us to get them witnesses. Lots of witnesses. But most of the people who come on our tours are from other countries – they're tourists, that's the point! It doesn't matter if they get slapped from one side of Greyfriars to the other – if they're going to be in Lapland a few days later, they're no use to us.'

'Aye, I know. Nobody from Edinburgh comes on the tour. Why would they? They live here.'

'Annie Carmichael and Sharon Brewster are the only two victims who live anywhere nearby and Sharon won't talk.'

'Annie?'

Ben shrugged. 'She's getting fed up of all the unwanted attention. She says that if she gives another interview, it will be the last time.'

Kate thought for a moment, absentmindedly rolling a cigarette. 'Sharon Ward came up from England for that last American TV feature, but I called and she doesn't want to talk any more. She said the press wouldn't leave her alone.'

'She's quite right.' Ben let out an exasperated sigh. 'These people don't want publicity. They only talk to the media because we ask them and then they get harassed or made fun of.'

Kate rummaged in her bag, pulled out a large red notebook and put it on the top of the bar. Its bright plastic cover looked out of place between the partners, both dressed head to foot in black. Ben wore a leather jacket, black jeans and engineer boots. Kate was dressed in a short black skirt, black boots and a black top. A full-length black leather coat was draped over the back of her stool. In the midst of the chattering students with their khaki combat trousers and brightly coloured shirts the guides stuck out a mile, yet they didn't seem dressed in this sombre style as a fashion statement or to attract attention. They had the air of people who had gone for a drink after a day at work; their clothes simply reflected the line they happened to be in. Death.

Kate opened the notebook. 'Right. Let's see what we've had recently.' She took out a pen, flicked through the pages and began to read.

'January the second. Jennifer Hackett complained of feeling something touching her in the Black Mausoleum. She tried to leave the tomb but collapsed in the doorway. She was taken outside and revived. I didn't get her phone number.'

'Why not?'

'Because she was unconscious.'

Kate marked a cross beside the entry. 'She was really shaken, she just wanted out of the cemetery as fast as possible. Anyway, she said she was from California so that's no use.'

'I know, babe. Who's next?'

'March the third. My tour.'

'Nothing at all for February?' Ben frowned and peered at the book, as if this shocking lack of supernatural activity were somehow an administrative error on Kate's part. Kate met his accusing stare with a look of indifference.

'Ben, at the moment we only do three tours a week. It's February. It's freezing. There's nobody to get attacked. Can I go on?'

'Please do.'

'Right. March the third. Whole bunch of the people in the vault started shouting that the temperature at the back had suddenly shot down. On the way out, some said they saw that white figure behind them.' She read down. 'But . . . they were from Australia. No use.'

Ben pulled a cigarette packet from his pocket and shook one loose in a burst of exasperation. It shot into the air and vanished over the bar. He looked around to make sure nobody had been watching. 'What is this white figure, anyway?' he said, annoyed. 'How come nobody on my tour ever sees any white figure? Do you think it's a dog?'

'Not unless it's on stilts.'

'A homeless guy?'

'That's hardly going to be a white figure, is it? You can't see your face two feet in front of you, it's so dark in that graveyard. If it's a homeless guy he's wearing a glow-in-the-dark body stocking.'

'Right. I'm glad nobody sees *that* on my tours. What's next? You want a pint?'

'Aye, please, love.'

'Two pints of lager.' Ben glanced at the figure pouring the drinks; he seemed familiar somehow, but Kate tugged at Ben's arm before he could get a second look.

'Here we go. March the fourth. A woman in her twenties insisted that something invisible was tugging at her leg. The spot she indicated was incredibly cold to the touch.'

'Boring.'

'True. Right. March the thirty-first. Catherine Greig claimed something was touching her face in the Black Mausoleum. When you shone the flashlight on her there was a handprint on her cheek, just like something had gripped her face.'

'That was a cracking one!' Ben smiled at the memory. 'But she didn't want to talk about it. Some people just don't know how to enjoy themselves.'

'April the twenty-second. My tour. A Mr Richardson complained of an agonising pain in his head. I remember that. He staggered out of the vault and collapsed outside.'

'What was his first name?'

'Mr.'

'Great.'

'Doesn't matter. He was American. Was going back to the US a couple of days later. No use.'

'May the sixteenth, Derek's tour. A female visitor collapsed in the Black Mausoleum.'

'Did he get her name?'

'She was taken away in an ambulance.'

'Damn!'

Kate looked at the page and began to read again.

'May the nineteenth. Chandra Markham suddenly felt freezing cold. Collapsed just outside the Black Mausoleum. Quite willing to be interviewed.'

'Yes!'

'She also lives in California.'

The barman put their pints down beside them and began to wipe the bar with a towel. He seemed to be trying his best to hear their conversation, but Ben and Kate were too wrapped up in the business at hand to notice.

'May the twentieth.' Kate tapped the page again and read. 'Jan Reese felt something freezing cold touching her head. Her face stayed numb with cold for some hours afterwards.'

Ben's face split into a grin.

'I called her. She'll talk and she actually lives in Scotland. Just outside Aberdeen. She'll come to town and talk on TV as long as someone pays her train fare and she can get a babysitter for her kids.'

'Superb. Shame she didn't collapse though.'

Kate and Ben Scott's attitude towards the visitors had changed, though they hardly realised it. They weren't about to admit to the possibility that they might be leading people into danger, so the whole thing had become a gruesome game. They dressed in long black leather coats like some entertainment Gestapo. They took people into the graveyard and whatever happened, happened. They were just doing their job.

'May the twenty-fifth, my tour.' Kate took a gulp of her pint. 'We got into the tomb and all of a sudden there was a loud knocking noise in there with us.'

'Somebody kicking the wall?'

'No. It seemed to come from all around.'

'Boring.'

'Well this is a great one. May the twenty-eighth, multiple sighting. At least six people felt cold spots and two of them had scratches on their body after the tour. The rapping noises were in the tomb again and this time they came from the roof!'

'Don't tell me. The entire tour was from Outer Mongolia.'

'Close enough. American, Australian and Dutch. June the eighteenth, a Danielle Ness claimed she heard voices whispering to her from the back of the Black Mausoleum, only there wasn't anyone behind her. Next day she had bruises down her leg.'

'USA?'

'USA.'

'Another one? Has the poltergeist got something against the locals?'

'It's certainly got a thing for Californians.' Kate put the cap back on her pen and tapped her lip. 'It's a month until the next TV crew get here; something's bound to happen before that.' She pointed the pen at Ben and made little jabbing motions. 'We have to start getting the names and addresses of everyone this thing goes after. Every single one.'

This was another change. Despite their disbelief, Ben and Kate now described the poltergeist in terms of a predatory entity, rather than a collection of odd phenomena. They talked of 'attacks' rather than 'incidents'.

Ben took an angry drag on his cigarette and spurted a stream of smoke across the bar. It sailed into the face of the barman, who was leaning over to get a better look at what was written in the notebook. He recoiled, coughing.

'Why do we have to take their names and addresses? We're a ghost tour, not a bloody investigation into the half-baked side of life.'

'We need proper proof.'

'Proof of what?'

Kate tilted her head to one side and brushed a strand of hair out of her mouth. She picked up the notebook and held it up. 'It seems to come in spurts. Nothing for a month or two, then all hell breaks loose.'

'A very apt metaphor.'

'You've got to admit, this is pretty weird, Ben.'

'Aye,' Ben sighed and rubbed his eyes. 'I know.'

'You're tired.' Kate reached out and put an affectionate hand on Ben's shoulder. The pen jabbed in his ear. 'Sorry.'

'S'all right. I am tired.'

Though City of the Dead was successful, it was far too small a business to support both Ben and Kate. Consequently Ben worked full time in an office as well as running the tours.

'I know. It's not easy working all day, then being one of only two tour guides at night.'

Ben patted her hand. 'It can't be easy for you either, being a full-time student and having to go to one lecture a week.'

Kate's eyes flashed. 'I work bloody hard at college, and you know it!'

Ben couldn't tell if she was genuinely annoyed, but he looked apologetic just in case. 'Anyway, there are three tour guides,' he corrected.

'Two.' It was Kate's turn to look apologetic. 'Derek's leaving. It's just you and me again.'

Ben rubbed his eyes once more.

'What for? It wasn't those cuts, was it?' Derek had finished a tour the week before with scratches on his body that he could not remember acquiring.

'No. He got a job working with computers. He loves working with computers.' Kate's expression indicated that she thought working with computers was as much fun as working with sewage.

'Great.' Ben rubbed his whole face to emphasise just how tired this new development would make him. 'Now we need to find a new tour guide.'

'Excuse me.' The barman leaned over. He had an open face, very young, topped with a thick tuft of black hair. 'If you're looking for a new tour guide, I'm the very person you want. I'd love to do something like that.' The barman smiled. He had an easy, friendly quality and, whether it was genuine or not, Ben and Kate recognised it immediately. Likeability – a tour guide's greatest asset.

'Let me get you another drink,' the barman said. 'It's on me.' He turned and fetched glasses.

'A free beer,' Kate hissed. 'He's hired.'

The barman glanced back. 'It's Ben and Kate, isn't it?'

'Yeah. And I *know* you,' Ben wagged a finger. 'You used to be the barman down at Bannerman's bar. In Niddry Street.'

The barman nodded and held out his hand. 'I did. Yes. Name's David Pollock.'

Roy

Written statement by Roy Hutchison, an electrician from Leeds, England. Roy was in the Covenanters' Prison on 15 November 2000.

I have never been interested in the supernatural and tend to think it's all a lot of rubbish. I came on the City of the Dead tour because I was interested in the history of Edinburgh and of Greyfriars, and I enjoyed that part. The supernatural stuff was well done, I suppose, and the stories were good fun but, as I said, there was no way I was going to believe in any of it.

In the Black Mausoleum my girlfriend, Joan, was getting all nervous and I thought to myself again how daft it was that people acted that way in the dark. Everyone was very close together because there were only about ten of us and I was standing on the right-hand side. Then something very cold grabbed my hand and let go again. At least, that's exactly what it felt like and it wasn't Joan because she was holding my other arm with both hands. There was nobody else near enough to touch me. I jumped but didn't say anything. I thought it had to be a trick, but I couldn't work out how it was done. When I came out of the vault I looked at my hand. There was a two-inch cut down the back of it. Not a scratch – a deep cut, which was bleeding badly. Later I took a photograph of it.

I have gone over and over this in my mind. Though I am totally reluctant to say that this was something supernatural, I can come up with absolutely no logical explanation for how it could have happened.

And . . . Cut!

There is no doubt that there is something supernatural . . .
I felt it myself.

MACIEJ TROJANOWSKI, PRESENTER, *UNBELIEVABLE*, POLISH NATIONAL TV, JULY 2000

Maciej Trojanowski and his television crew set up their cameras outside the Black Mausoleum. The light was fading fast but they had two portable, battery-operated lights and were attaching them to tripods outside the door of the tomb. Maciej and the crew had flown over from Poland to film an episode of their popular national show, *Unbelievable*, the subject of this particular unbelievable episode being the Mackenzie Poltergeist. In the morning they had taken in the sights and sounds of Edinburgh, shooting the Old Town's stunning medieval skyline and a few narrow wynds for inclusion in their show. Then they went to Greyfriars to interview Ben Scott and some of the poltergeist victims.

It had been a beautiful July day. The sun streamed from a cloudless sky, the graveyard trees were crammed with glossy olive leaves and flowers sprouted carelessly in patches of soil between headstones. The north-eastern slope of the graveyard even had a heat haze and the tallest tombstones shimmered as though they were halfway between this world and a more mystical one. Maciej and Jan sat on the grass in their shirtsleeves and matching sunglasses listening to the birds. A hundred yards away a family were wandering between the graves. Now and then the mother would point to a particularly intricate gravestone and a child would run, laughing, from a skull carved into some shadowy recess. The shouts of pupils at play in the Heriot School grounds drifted on the sunny air over the graveyard wall. At the gates of the Covenanters' Prison, the three-strong Polish crew – who appeared to be called Jan, Jan and Jan – were filming one of the poltergeist victims, also called Jan.

In these beautiful surroundings, with the air hot and the breeze calming, the city out of sight and very nearly out of mind, it was hard to imagine that anything bad could happen here. On a day like this it was hard to imagine that anything bad could happen anywhere.

Maciej Trojanowski, the presenter of *Unbelievable*, was a tall, imposing figure with a balding head and a rangy, athletic physique. He was a direct man with a direct stare and, every time they talked, Ben felt he should keep checking there wasn't some dirty mark on his face that Maciej was examining. Ben liked Maciej Trojanowski. His name was pronounced 'Magic', or something very close, and there was a touch of that about his demeanour; his companionship seemed somehow both comforting and slightly frightening. Ben realised it was like meeting the teacher he had feared most at school, only now he was 37 and able to handle it. Almost.

'So,' Maciej said sternly. 'Do you have an explanation for what is going on in this graveyard?'

'No. I have no idea.'

'That will not do for the TV show.'

'Sorry.'

Sentences sounded funny coming from this large, austere man. The presenter's grasp of English was excellent, but his diction was clipped and the words distorted by his thick Polish accent. It suddenly occurred to Ben that Maciej sounded like Count Dracula. He could see the tall Pole rising from behind a grave, silk cloak trailing behind, scaring the living daylights out of passing tours by shouting 'I am vun off de Undaaaaaaaaaahd!'

'The graveyard's been a bit disappointing recently,' Ben said. 'We've gone all the way through June, one of our busiest months, and not a thing. Not a peep. Nobody felt funny. No cuts. No collapses. We've just finished training a new tour guide, David Pollock. We told him all about the creepy things that happen in here. He's going to think we're idiots.'

'Well, we will shoot in the Black Mausoleum tonight. Perhaps the poltergeist will be caught on film.'

'Oh, I'm sure it will.' Ben couldn't have sounded less sincere if he had been promising the poltergeist would sing a few numbers from *The Sound of Music.*

Now it was 11.00 p.m. but not particularly dark. Edinburgh was on roughly the same latitude as Moscow and its northern setting meant that even at a late hour the summer sky was deep blue rather than black. Of course, the city made up for this in the winter months by looking like the middle of the night from 3.00 p.m. onwards. In the Covenanters' Prison, the camera crew had finished setting up their equipment and were talking softly to each other in Polish. The burning embers of their cigarettes flickered and jumped in the dark at every gesture accompanying their words. They leaped to their feet at the sound of the approaching tour.

At the other end of the prison, David unlocked the gates and led his whispering tour party down the dark passage of tombs towards the cameras. The visitors blinked and winced as they passed through the harsh light of the spots, only to be plunged into the darkness of the Black Mausoleum. Once they were all inside the tomb David launched into his favourite story and the camera crew began lugging equipment back towards the gate for a long shot of the tour emerging from the vault.

'We will not take the camera into the tomb, no,' Maciej had explained to Ben that afternoon. 'We are a small unit with only one camera. We do not wish the poltergeist to break it.'

Ben looked at him quizzically. With that accent it was hard to tell when Maciej was joking. Maciej kept a poker face. 'No. What it is . . . we do not want to spoil the atmosphere for your paying visitors. And we do not want one of them to panic and knock over our cameramen and lights. This is possible, no?'

'It is definitely possible. Yes.'

'Then we will wait outside. When the tour is finished with this Black Mausoleum, we will ask some of the party to go back in and we will film then.'

'Good luck persuading them to go in twice.'

Maciej gave a dismissive wave of his hand. 'It is television,' he said grandly. 'Everyone wants to be on television. Especially on Polish television.'

Ben Scott smiled again. He liked Maciej Trojanowski.

Suddenly there was a scream and a collective gasp from inside the Black Mausoleum. The startled film crew spun round to face the way they had come. David Pollock's head popped round the side of the tomb door, his expression of surprise turning to one of annoyance as he spotted the faraway Poles. 'What are you doing up there with the camera?' he admonished. 'We've got a collapse!'

The woman who had gone down was a student visiting from France, Christine Deveraux. She had suddenly become freezing cold in the vault and the next thing she remembered was waking up outside. David had acted quickly and efficiently, delegating the four tour members who looked least terrified to carry the stricken girl out of the tomb. The guides faced a dilemma over collapses; each was trained in emergency first aid and knew that an unconscious person shouldn't be moved, but they also knew that a frightened crowd was a danger to a prone victim, and that the filthy floor of a pitch-black vault was the worst place for someone unconscious to be lying. So, once they had checked the person was breathing, the tour guide gently moved any collapsed person the few feet it took to reach the grass and cool air outside. Invariably the victim woke up as soon as they were taken out, just as those who fled, terrified or nauseous, felt better as soon as they exited the tomb. Christine Deveraux was no exception and opened her eyes almost immediately. As soon as she was able to stand, the television crew led the shaking girl to one side, firing excited questions at her – which she couldn't understand because they were talking in Polish.

'Well, Mackenzie,' David said to the empty tomb, his heart beating fast. 'I get to meet you at last . . . You're quite a showman too.'

David led his party, now very quiet, from the Covenanters' Prison to the cemetery exit and was bidding them goodnight when Maciej Trojanowski strode over, balding pate glistening in the moonlight. He had Christine Deveraux in tow.

'Wonderful,' he said happily to the assembled crowd. 'Now, if we could take you all back into the tomb for a few minutes, we will film a re-enactment of what happened.'

'You've got to be kidding!' David looked at him wide-eyed. The tour party seemed to share his opinion.

'It will be exciting. No?'

'That's one way of putting it.'

'Come, ladies and gentlemen.' Maciej turned his considerable charm on the group. 'You will be on national television.' He indicated Christine Deveraux. 'Even this young lady is willing to go back in and act out the scene for us again. She is brave, yes?'

Maciej had obviously worked his charm on Christine, though the young French girl looked more resigned than heroic. Not only was she going back to face the Mackenzie Poltergeist, she was also going to have to take another nosedive onto the dirty tomb floor.

'People! Who will come with me?' Maciej sounded like Moses setting off for the Promised Land.

A group of about five came forward, giggling nervously.

'This will do, yes,' said Maciej, smiling broadly.

The re-enactment must have been one of the fastest shoots in cinema history. David herded the small group, along with the cameramen, back into the Black Mausoleum. Christine Deveraux fell down and everyone left the vault at a brisk trot, carrying the fallen Frenchwoman a lot less carefully than they had last time.

'Cut!' said Maciej Trojanowski, with a flourish. The tour party dropped Christine and instinctively checked their arms and hands in case the Pole was referring to any marks there.

Christine Deveraux turned out to be made of stern stuff after all for, a few days later, she turned up on Ben Scott's tour. But her resolve did not last. As Ben opened the gates to the

Covenanters' Prison, he noticed that she was no longer with the group. He did not see her again.

Wilson Chapel stood in his garden with a hammer in his hand and looked at the shed he had built. He should have been pleased; it might not be a big shed but it was sturdy and well made. For some reason, though, Wilson really didn't like it. It wasn't the building itself, he thought. It was where he had been forced to put it. The garden wasn't large, and the left-hand corner was the only logical place a structure like that would fit. For months there had been a pile of debris piled on that very spot and Wilson had never quite got round to shifting it. Now he didn't have to. Two weeks ago the whole lot had gone up in flames, a blaze so severe that three fire engines had been called to battle it and Wilson and his partner Angela had been forced to flee their home.

No . . . it wasn't the shed Wilson disliked, it was what was right behind it; the little wooden structure was built against the garden wall and on the other side was Greyfriars Kirkyard. A visitor to the house would not have been able to tell this, for the wall was much too high to see over, were there not one obvious clue – rising above the barrier, topped with its ugly fat acorn of stone, was the mausoleum of George Mackenzie. It towered over the shed like a mocking shadow, ancient, impressive and sinister and, no matter where the sun stood in the sky, the little wooden building always seemed to be in its shade.

Wilson sat on the garden bench and drank a mug of tea. Through the kitchen window he could see Angela pouring herself a cup, unaware that he was looking at her. Yet she *had* complained of being watched several times, not by Wilson, but by something she couldn't quite see – something she was sure stared through the window at her whenever she was alone.

This conviction had begun right after the fire, though Angela was not the type to give in to flights of fancy and neither was Wilson. He was a mechanic, a man who took things apart and put them together again until he knew exactly what was wrong. He wasn't sure what was wrong with the shed. All he knew was that he too got an uneasy sensation whenever he was inside.

Never mind. He was a practical man and he knew the feeling would pass.

A few days after the Polish TV crew had gone, the US Discovery channel crew arrived to shoot their version of the poltergeist tale. Once again, Ben Scott and Kate Kavanagh found themselves back in Greyfriars telling their story.

'If I spend any more time in here with film crews I'm going to get a chair with my name on the back,' Ben muttered.

Kate was lying full length on a flat tomb, hair fanned out around her face, soaking up the sun. Dressed all in black for the cameras, she looked more like a devil worshipper than a sun worshipper, or a vampire who hadn't made it back to her coffin before dawn caught her. Kate didn't care. In her mind, heaven had sand and deckchairs and was somewhere off the coast of Greece.

'Stop complaining, love,' she said lazily. 'It's a beautiful day and you've got away from your daytime work and out into the fresh air.'

'The sun gives me a headache.'

'That's called a hangover, Ben.'

This crew was going for a larger shoot than the small Polish unit could manage and the skeletons of tripods and frames were strewn around the gates of the Covenanters' Prison. Several costumes were hung neatly on tombstones.

'They're filming enactments of Covenanters being persecuted by George Mackenzie,' Ben complained. 'Like that has anything to do with anything! I told them the poltergeist wasn't named after George Mackenzie, that it's named after his tomb because that's where the first attack took place. What do they care?'

Kate stretched happily and yawned. 'I think the costumes look nice,' she said, knowing this would annoy Ben even more. It worked.

'The Covenanters are dressed in monks' robes!' he ranted.

'What would people who hate Catholics be doing dressed like Friar Tuck? And there's only four of them.'

'I don't think they can afford to pay 1,200 extras just to satisfy your need for accuracy.'

'The guy dressed as Mackenzie looks like a judge.'

'George Mackenzie was a judge.'

'Not in some bad TV sitcom.'

Kate pointed languidly to where two backpackers were sitting eating a sandwich, a tranquil enough picture were it not for the fact that both seemed to be bleeding from severe head wounds. 'They're re-enacting a couple of poltergeist attacks too. That's quite good.'

'I know. I saw them filming it.' Ben wasn't about to stop his tirade. It was making his hangover feel better. 'The entire McDonald's franchise doesn't have that much ketchup. The Mackenzie Poltergeist scratches people, it doesn't tear them limb from limb. It was like watching *The Texas Chainsaw Massacre.*'

Kate rolled over to expose her other side to the sun. 'I know, love. Why don't you go and tell them how to do it properly?'

'Aye. I'll go see what the Cecil B. De Mille gang are up to now.' Ben shouldered his leather jacket and sloped off to the Covenanters' Prison, where Jan Reese and Annie Carmichael, two of the poltergeist victims, were being interviewed.

Jan Reese was sitting on the grass opposite the Black Mausoleum. A small woman in her mid-thirties with liquid brown eyes, she looked a little like Sue-Ellen from the soap opera *Dallas*. She also looked pale and shaken.

Ben stopped. 'You went back into the Black Mausoleum for your interview, didn't you?'

Jan nodded an affirmative. Maciej Trojanowski had interviewed her the week before, but even his powers of persuasion hadn't been enough to get her back inside the tomb. This time, it seemed, she had relented.

'Wish you hadn't?'

Jan nodded again. Then she burst into a sunny smile, laughing at her own foolishness, or just enjoying being out of the tomb and back in the light. Across from her, the Black Mausoleum looked as grainy as a faded photograph, the interior a squat hole that had never felt a ray of sun.

Ben patted Jan on the shoulder and walked a little further to where Dan the American director was talking to Annie Carmichael. The camera crew were taking a break, scattered around the Covenanter's Prison with the rest of the equipment and sipping coffees from polystyrene containers.

Annie Carmichael was a tall, slim woman, well dressed with short dark hair and, like Jan Reese, had striking eyes, this time faded cobalt blue. As Ben walked past he could hear her describing her experience to the director. 'I was standing in the vault when I suddenly felt cold,' Annie was saying in a cultured voice. 'It seemed that something was touching the back of my head. Then, when I got out of the tomb, someone noticed that I had a cut down the back of my neck.'

'Well, I'll be damned!'

Dan sounded genuinely bowled over. Ben smiled to himself. Americans. You had to love them. He turned back, intending to point out that the Mackenzie Poltergeist was capable of far more spectacular stuff than one cut. The director beckoned to him, eyes wide. 'Willya take a look at this,' he said as Ben walked over. There was a red weal down the back of Annie Carmichael's neck. 'That wasn't there a second ago,' Dan said in puzzlement. 'I was watching and it suddenly appeared.' He looked anxiously around. 'Where's the damned camera?' He turned and waved violently at the camera crew. They sipped their coffee and waved happily back.

'Don't bother,' said Ben. 'It's gone again.'

It had. Suddenly there was no blemish on Annie's shapely neck. Ben was almost convinced he had imagined it. The director looked at him, a mixture of puzzlement and disbelief in his eyes.

Ben shrugged.

'Loves attention. Doesn't love the camera.'

Annie Carmichael gave no more interviews.

David

David Pollock is a tour guide taking visitors into Greyfriars Graveyard. He has done so since June 2000. This statement was taken in March 2001.

The first genuinely spooky event on my tours was in July 2000 and I'll probably remember it for the rest of my life. After it happened, I even thought about quitting my job, though I'm glad I didn't. I've met many interesting people and though I can't explain the things I've seen, I now think it is great that I've seen them.

It was early July and a nice Scottish night – the wind was howling and it was freezing. We were making the best of optimum tour conditions, 'we' being about 35 visitors and myself. We were having a pretty good time, laughing and joking. Then we entered the tomb. I set the scene with a few creepy stories. I couldn't really tell them much about the poltergeist, as I hadn't yet done many tours, but I noticed that there was suddenly a very definite change amongst the party. Before there had been some good-natured heckling, now there was only the occasional nervous giggle, or an over-loud guffaw from one of the more image-conscious Australian blokes. The entire tour moved closer together. I was quite pleased. I thought it was me.

To crank up the scary-juice a bit, I switched off my torch, the only source of illumination in the tomb. With the sudden plunge into darkness, there came a bizarre deadening of my voice. I noticed it immediately and so did the crowd; it was like someone had turned off the echo in a sound chamber. My voice is loud anyway and in the tomb it's even easier to hear. But now, instead of impressing the tourists with my storytelling ability, I sounded as though I was talking through a gas mask. Weird. I was so astonished I even stopped speaking, and that doesn't happen very often.

I restarted my tale, this time pacing backwards and forwards. The tour was listening more to the sounds than the words, which normally would have ticked me off, but now I was doing it as well. It seemed like there were dead spots in various points in the tomb, places that squashed the sound flat. OK, I thought. What's one more quirk in the world's most haunted tour? Kate and Ben had told me to expect weird things, and the crowd was certainly impressed. Bring it on, I thought – the more they're scared the bigger they tip.

Suddenly a deep low noise was emitted from the wall of the tomb. It sounded like a groan of pain. The noise rose in volume for perhaps 20 seconds then cut off. There was silence apart from the breathing of the crowd. Some people seemed afraid, some were just blank – and the rest were trying to figure out how I had done it.

There was nobody standing anywhere near the source of the groan, including me. I brushed it off with a joke. 'Sorry. Must have been something I ate.'

What else could I do?

The faces relaxed, but I was starting to feel really strange and things were definitely not under my control. That's no way for a tour guide to feel and when one member suggested we finish as quickly as possible and go to the nearest bar instead, I was in full agreement. Soon we were out of the wind and ensconced around the fire of Greyfriars pub.

The first topic up for discussion was, of course, what went on in the tomb. I discovered that although roughly half the tour party had heard exactly what I had and were twice as freaked, the other half had heard nothing at all. I found myself talking to a big Glaswegian. He had muscles like balloons and looked as hard as steel-toe. I remembered seeing him at the back wall of the tomb. 'Aye, I spent the hale time standing at the back. And that's whar the noise came frae. A big groan, ken, like some dude's had a serious hiding. I'm actually in charge o' maintenance fir the largest cemetery in Scotland. And let me tell ye ah've never bin sae afraid in ma life as I was an hour ago.'

I was on my way to Canada at the end of July and the final tour before my trip was a busy one – over 50, due to the fact that I'd miscalculated tour numbers.

We reached the prison gates. I gave my usual warning, undid the padlock and everyone went in. As soon as one man walked through the gates he started sobbing hysterically then collapsed unconscious on the ground. His friends tried to bring him round, but it was not until we carried him out of the prison that he became anything like coherent.

'You all right mate? Anything hurt? No broken bones?' I tried to be as sympathetic as possible, especially since the victim was six foot tall. 'Had a few to drink, eh?'

'No. Nothing at all. I've got my car with me! What the hell just happened?'

I had to admit I didn't have a clue. He tried to stand but his legs were having none of it, especially since the direction they were supposed to go was farther into the Covenanters' Prison. He refused point blank to be checked out medically, but allowed his mates to help him back to his car. That was the last I saw of them.

I was told in no uncertain terms that 24 people would go no further, and they strode off en masse towards the graveyard exit. In a way that was pretty handy because, when I took the rest to the Black Mausoleum, there was now room for them all. 'Well, folks, I guess that leaves just us. And the ghost.' I figure it never does any harm to crank it up a notch. However, after five minutes in the tomb, there had been several complaints about cold spots and people being touched and one blood-curdling scream from a woman at the back.

'Shall we just leave?' I finally asked.

'Hell, yes!' said the crowd.

Canada was singing sweetly to me.

I actually went to my boss, Ben, and told him I was thinking of quitting. Ben can be very persuasive. I stayed.

It was quite a start to my tour guide career.

There have been other 'incidents' since then, but that first month was really something. I wonder sometimes how much I miss as well. Two young American girls met Kate at the tour sign and told her they had been grabbed in the Black Mausoleum by 'cold invisible hands'. They now sported an array of bruises around their upper arms and thighs. I had done the tour and hadn't even noticed that anything was going on.

Oh yes. I've had seven more people collapsing due to cold spots.

It's not me.

Honest.

The Pheromone Theory

No one has been able to offer an explanation for these
attacks, but local newspapers took photographs of some
of the victims, who reported deep cuts and bruises . . .
Many wonder why this evil creature assaults and attacks
some visitors and not others – but the tour guides have
their own theory.

'HAUNTED HISTORY: EDINBURGH', THE US HISTORY CHANNEL, 22 SEPTEMBER 2000

Ben Scott moved into his graveyard dwelling in the summer of
2000. It was coincidence that he had found a place with a view
over Greyfriars, not a morbid desire to look down on death, and
it was undeniably handy for the tours. The flat was part of the
eighteenth-century tenements in Candlemaker Row. From the
street it was necessary to climb four flights of spiral stairs to
reach Ben's front door. Walk through the apartment, however,
and the two latticed windows looked out over a headstone-
dotted vista only seven feet below. There was even a tomb built
into the wall directly underneath the windowsill.

Some of Ben's friends had expressed misgivings about his
choice of location. One of them, looking across the maze of
graves, voiced what many visitors secretly thought. 'It would
give me the creeps staying here.' She wrinkled her nose, as if she
could smell corpses. 'Doesn't it give you the creeps?'

'It's just a big garden,' said Ben. 'Only, filled with dead
people.'

All the same, he made it a rule never to watch a horror film
if he was going to be sleeping alone.

David Pollock sat on the window seat in Ben's new apartment.
He looked unhappy and fidgeted with his short beard. Only 21,

David's youthful face had prompted him to grow a goatee in an attempt to make himself appear older. Now he didn't look a day under 17.

Night was falling on the city of the dead outside and the sky was darkening through the panes behind him. He had drank tea with Ben and chatted, but Ben wasn't much for chatting and David obviously had something else on his mind. Through the window the tombstones slowly faded and David's reflection strengthened on the glass, until the two images blended into a macabre Maigrit figure with headstones for medals.

David Pollock was worried. A natural showman, he had been delighted to discover that he could scare people with his powers of oration. He had been delighted when Christine Deveraux collapsed on his tour in front of a TV crew. He had even been delighted at the prospect of being on Polish national television, even if the programme had called him Ben Scott by mistake. But he had not been delighted at the events of the last month.

A few days after the Polish shoot, on 14 July, an American radio operator named Kyle Plackmeyer claimed to have been attacked in the Black Mausoleum by what he took to be the Mackenzie Poltergeist. It was David's tour. Four days later David and a few of his tour party heard a low growling coming from the vault wall. Less than a week after that, there was a multiple sighting; three women – Austrian, Irish and Serbian, and all strangers to each other – panicked when they felt something brushing against their faces. The sensations they felt were accompanied by a sudden and extreme drop in the temperature of the vault. It was David's tour. Four days later a man collapsed as David reached the gates of the Covenanters' Prison. It was the first collapse to happen outside the Black Mausoleum since the tours began.

On 29 July, one week later, Charity Pirkle from the US was hit in the side by something she could not see and then felt something she likened to a man's hand in a thick glove grabbing her foot. David Pollock was the tour guide.

David was worried.

'I don't know if I should quit the tours,' he said eventually.

The windows behind him were now black. 'I don't know if I'm doing something wrong.'

Judging by the incredible frequency of incidents on David's tours, Ben Scott had no doubt that his new tour guide was doing something very right. As company director he leapt into action. 'Have a beer,' he said.

'No thanks.'

'Right. Glass of wine it is.' He marched into the kitchen and opened the fridge. There were four bottles of Sauvignon Blanc and half a pound of cheese.

'My parents are quite religious, you know?' David continued. 'They think that exploiting the dead is a pretty bad thing.'

'What do they want you to do?' Ben emerged from the kitchen with a bottle and two half-pint glasses. 'Dig a hole at the end of each tour and drop in a percentage?' He fought for a while with a cheap plastic corkscrew that bent every time he pushed it into the cork.

'I talked to my girlfriend about it too,' David said. 'She's freaked out. Am I disturbing something I shouldn't?'

'Think of it this way.' Ben put on his most reasonable voice. 'Every day there's guys out in Greyfriars on their lunch hour, eating pizza and using those flat gravestones as tables.' He gave up on the corkscrew and attacked the cork with a screwdriver. 'There's one over there catches a lot of sun and it's got a wee hole in it where you can put your juice.' The screwdriver shot into the bottle and a little spout of wine bubbled over Ben's fingers. 'There are schoolkids from Heriot use the cemetery as a shortcut. At night you even get homeless guys sleeping there.'

'You do?'

'Well. No. Not since the poltergeist thing started.'

Ben filled the half-pint glasses with wine and got off that particular subject.

'Listen. St Giles' Cathedral, down on the Royal Mile, it used to have a graveyard,' he said. 'So did St Leonards. Now one's a car park and the other is a police station. It's no big deal.'

David brightened a little at this. Then he remembered why

he felt so bad in the first place. 'When I started, you and Kate told me about all the things that happened on the tours. And you said not much ever happened to Derek.'

'Not much.' Ben thought back. 'He's the only one who ever got cut, if that's any help.'

'So most incidents happened on your and Kate's tours.'

'True.'

'How many attacks have you had on your tours in the month since I started?'

Ben Scott thought carefully.

'Ehm . . . none.'

'On Kate's?'

'Oooh. I'd say about . . . hmmm . . .'

'None?'

'Yeah. None.'

David took a couple of large gulps and began to roll a cigarette before plunging back into the fray.

'In the last month I've had six attacks on my tours.' He licked a cigarette paper and peered over the top at Ben. 'These are the big ones I'm talking about, I'm not counting all the people who just refused to go in or felt spooked.'

Ben raised his glass in salute.

'You're certainly heading for our employee of the month certificate.'

David saluted him back, but he still looked troubled.

'What if there really is something in there, Ben? Something bad.'

'If there is, it likes you just fine.'

'That's what I mean.' David lit his cigarette and shook the match furiously, animated now that a doorway had been opened to the idea lurking at the back of his mind. 'All of a sudden it's like it switched from you to me. It's like I'm some kind of . . . I don't know. A *focus*.'

Ben winced inwardly at David's choice of phrase, though he had been thinking exactly the same thing.

'I'm not bothered about cuts and scratches or even people falling down,' David said gamely. 'But what if I make it stronger?

What if it's something evil and I help it to get . . . what? Get out? Get bigger? I don't know.'

'David. You are not going to be attacked by a poltergeist on a ghost tour. Honestly.'

David only shrugged. 'You don't know for sure though, do you?' He took another big gulp of wine. 'I heard a laugh in that tomb! It's not all tourists' imaginations. You haven't got a good explanation for what's happening.'

'Actually, I have,' Ben said proudly. 'Nothing to do with demons or spirits or electromagnets or psychokinesis or all that nonsense either. I made it up myself.'

'You've been thinking about it then?' David smiled.

'My house looks into a cemetery famous for an active poltergeist. I piss it off every night by taking visitors to gawk round its home. If it does exist, it probably holds a bit of a grudge against me personally.' Ben moved David out of the way and pulled the blind down. 'You'd be surprised at the things I think about.'

Then he told David Pollock his Pheromone Theory.

Pheromones (pronounced 'fair-uh-moans') are types of hormones, chemicals that living organisms release in order to communicate with other members of their own species. In many ways pheromones are more effective than sight or sound signals, for they do not fade quickly and are effective over a long range. The first pheromone was discovered in 1952 and was found in the glands of female silkworm moths. Called 'bombykol', the substance could attract male moths over huge distances. The scientist Lewis Thomas wrote in *The Lives of A Cell*:

> It has been soberly calculated that if a single female moth were to release all the bombykol in her sac in a single spray, all at once, she could theoretically attract a trillion males in that instant.

Insect pheromones, as well as attracting the opposite sex, have other functions. Ants can lay down a 'trail pheromone' that attracts and guides other ants to any food they have found. But more importantly, when an ant is attacked or disturbed it can release an 'alarm pheromone'. This type of pheromone is detected by other ants in the area and makes them extremely agitated. They, too, begin to release alarm pheromones, making the cumulative distress stronger and spreading it farther, and they continue to do so until the danger has gone. Ants are hardly the most emotional creatures on the earth, but what they are creating is little more than chemically induced fear.

A 1971 study by scientist Martha McClintock suggested that human pheromones might be responsible for the strange phenomenon whereby human females living together developed synchronised menstrual cycles. In 1986, she was proved right when Dr Winifred Cutler of the Athena Institute documented positive existence of pheromones in humans. It may be an old myth, but it seems that there really is a physical, sexual chemistry between people.

If that is true, there may be other types of undetected pheromone chemistry between human beings. As Martha McLintock wrote:

> In other species there are many other types of pheromones, not dependent on ovarian function . . . well-controlled studies of humans are now needed to determine whether there are other types of pheromones with effects that are as far-reaching in humans as they are in other species.

Pheromones may explain the extreme behaviour that is often observed in large groups of people. Mass hysteria, mass indoctrination, mass violence – all might be the result of pheromones spreading through a group and influencing the individuals within that group. And, if there is an alarm pheromone in humans, it might be used to transmit fear in exactly the same way.

David looked impressed.

'That's an interesting theory.'

'Thank you. I'm working on turning base metals into gold next week.'

'I just don't see what it has to do with the poltergeist.'

Ben sighed and poured himself another glass of wine.

'Right. Consider this,' he said, in his best storytelling voice. 'Ants. Ants. With legs. And feet.'

He paused and looked at David expectantly.

'Yes. I get that part.'

'All right.' Ben tapped his glass against his teeth and thought for a second. 'Right. Imagine it's the '70s and you're going out clubbing. It was called the disco, in my day.'

'Did you have flares?'

'I was a punk rocker, but you're on the right track. Let's assume, for the sake of the theory, that I am the John Travolta type. I have on my best Crimpeine shirt and polyester trousers and all my friends come over in matching outfits, including your girlfriend because she wants me.'

David sighed.

'It's your theory.'

'Exactly. So . . . we all start dancing on my polypropylene carpet in our nylon socks.'

'I've been to parties like that.' David grinned.

'I don't want to know. Anyway. Put together all that shuffling around and man-made fibre and you can build up enough static electricity to power a Ford Capri. Then one of us gets out a comb and touches someone else. Bang!' Ben thumped the table loudly in the manner of a mad scientist.

'Ah,' David nodded slowly. 'Now I really don't understand where this is going.'

'OK,' Ben sighed. 'Imagine the same thing with pheromones. Get a group of people in an enclosed stone mausoleum every night. Make them afraid. They release alarm pheromones. These pheromones can't go anywhere, they build up in concentration – maybe even join with the emissions from the night before – and that makes the party release even more pheromones, until finally there's enough of a concentration to actually overcome a member of the tour party. It might make them hear things or feel cold or sick, or even knock them out. It could even cause a reaction that would mark their skin.'

David raised his eyebrows.

'Oh. I see.'

'It explains a lot of poltergeist lore. Poltergeists are associated with teenagers going through puberty or people going through the menopause. They're associated with people undergoing chemical hormonal changes. Nutty people. People with sexual problems.' He squinted at David. 'You got any sexual problems?'

'Not apart from being a sex addict.'

'Same here.'

They clinked glasses again and Ben continued: 'See, on the tour there are different people each night and some are more likely to produce pheromones, or succumb to them for that matter, than others. That's why there isn't an attack every night – the circumstances have to be right.' He pointed to himself with satisfaction. 'I'm a bit of a trigger. You're even stronger.'

David was nodding enthusiastically. 'So . . . when I go to Canada, things might start happening on your tours again.'

David was leaving Edinburgh in a few days' time and flying out to North America for his brother's wedding. He had decided this was a golden opportunity to stay and do nothing there for several weeks, and liked to remind everyone of that fact.

'Maybe.' Ben chose not to rise to the bait. 'It does all fit, though. Poltergeists are supposed to scare people, but they don't hurt them. Alarm pheromones are designed to do the same – just create a state of alarm.'

David's glass halted halfway to his lips. 'But the Mackenzie Poltergeist *does* hurt people.'

'Well, this is an extreme case.'

David thought some more. He turned and peered through a slat in the blind, even though there was nothing to see. 'You not noticed the way people collapse in the tomb?'

'Reluctantly?' But Ben knew exactly what David meant.

A high proportion of the visitors who collapsed in the Black Mausoleum didn't just fall down on the spot. They felt sick, or cold and overwhelmed, with a desire to get out of the vault and it was as they made for the tomb door that they went down. Anyone who collapsed where they had been standing usually had a barrier of people preventing them reaching the exit. Regardless of whether or not they made it to the door, all the victims had one thing in common; they were standing slightly apart from the rest of the group when they were 'attacked'.

'It's like this thing picks off people who stray too far away from the rest.' David finished his wine. 'Or separates them from the herd.'

'I hope you don't refer to visitors as "the herd" when you take them on tours.'

'Do you really believe it's just imagination?'

'More than I believe there's a devil in my back yard giving the new employee a hard time.'

'I suppose.' David stood up to go. Ben rose with him and patted his shoulder.

'So. You'll still be on the tours once you come back from Canada?'

David shook his hand.

'Aye, I suppose I will.'

'Good man. And David . . .'

'Yes?' David turned.

'Don't take the poltergeist with you on the plane. The pilot sits on his own.'

Claire

Statement given by Claire Valentine on 1 February 2001:

I moved into the flat on 7 January 2000, having read a little of the history of my building and found it fascinating; if you live in old Edinburgh you live hand in hand with the past, and it turned out that my building had been a poorhouse situated between the graveyard and the Bedlam Asylum! The only thing I found vaguely creepy about my new location was the Edinburgh University Artificial Intelligence building next door. Some of those students were genuinely disturbing.

The flat was light and airy, but quite small. Although built in 1752 it had been converted recently into modern apartments and was not the least dated inside. I did not know much about Jack, the former owner, only that he loved the flat and the area, and was extremely sad to be moving. Why go then?

It did not take long to settle into my new flat. It was my home, all mine (and the building society's, of course), and I finally had control of my own environment. There was no one else to take into consideration – no one to tidy up after, or moan about the mess I made. I didn't have to cook for anyone else – I didn't have to cook at all. I felt peaceful and secure. When I closed my door at night there was only me, and I loved it.

Maybe I should have taken more note of the things going on around me. Ronald, the 'quiet' guy from downstairs, was admitted into the locked ward of a psychiatric unit not long after I arrived.

One night, just after I moved in, a friend and I were sitting in the living-room chatting when the candles suddenly blew out. All 24 of them. Simultaneously. There were no open windows. No draught.

The next morning whilst getting ready for work, I searched desperately for the second of a pair of shoes, to no avail. Worried I would miss my bus I tossed the single one back into the cupboard, slammed the door and stuck my trainers on instead (very professional with a black suit). On my return that evening, I was pleasantly surprised to find the pair of shoes laid out for me by the bed. I thought it slightly odd, but the fact that I knew where they were was more important to me than how they got there. After all, my stereo hadn't vanished, so why worry?

Then, one July night, something happened that really disturbed my sense of safety and security. Lying in bed reading at the end of a hot, dry day, I heard the sound of hammering rain. Thinking this was strange, I pulled my blind up to take a peek. There were flames licking the windowsill – *my* windowsill! After dressing (almost) I ran from the flat, bolting out of the main door to be confronted by the deafening roar of the enormous blaze lunging from the archway under my flat.

It took three fire engines to extinguish the fire and rescue the two sheepdogs that lived downstairs (after being wrapped in blankets and given a whiff of oxygen, they didn't seem the least perturbed by their experience). The police were never able to establish the cause of the fire, only its point of origin. The garden of the flat under mine shared a wall with Greyfriars cemetery and the fire started in a pile of rubbish stacked there.

The fire seemed to kick-start a chain of strange occurrences not only in my own flat but in the flat of the couple next door. I would leave a glass on the floor at night and it would be in the kitchen when I got up in the morning. Arriving home from work I would find the right-hand door of my bathroom cabinet open – always the right-hand door – and my toothbrush gone. I might be a bit of a slob at times, but I do have a thing about shutting all the doors in the house, including cupboards, and the cabinet door can't swing open itself.

Small things, I know, but then in bed with my partner one night I realised I could hear a third person breathe! Now that was disturbing. Though my partner was asleep, someone seemed to be blowing raspberries in my ear. Next time the noise had moved to the bottom of the bedroom wall, near the door, and my partner swore it was not a raspberry but the sound of giggling.

A bedside light started buzzing and continued to do so after I had disconnected it from its power source. I came home one evening, let myself into the flat and heard what sounded like a hundred chattering voices that cut off abruptly with the slamming of the door. A month after British summertime had ended I was delighted to discover that the clock on the VCR had righted itself, though I had had no clue how to do it. Three separate watches stopped at ten to two. Doors opened and slammed shut independently. What was going on?

One Saturday afternoon I bumped into a neighbour who owned the flat with the garden (and the dogs). He invited me into the flat he shared with his partner for a cup of tea and we got chatting. Much to my surprise, Wilson and Angela had their own mysterious goings-on going on! Their 'supernatural' occurrences were similar to mine, but with a more sinister undertone; crockery moved, glasses smashed, lights went on and off.

I was beginning to feel genuinely spooked. Was I

just kidding myself about having control of my surrounding environment? Was I as alone in my home as I would like to believe? I had never felt anything sinister in my flat. I had never even believed in the existence of anything sinister to feel. Up to this point I had viewed the goings on in my home with bemusement rather than fear or concern. Now, however, I knew it was happening to my neighbours as well as me. The same thing was happening to other people. And worse.

I have never believed in the supernatural and the idea of ghosts and ghoulies has always seemed slightly ridiculous to me. However, I have no explanation for what has gone on in my home and as I write this I notice that my watch has started working again. I started writing at ten to two.

How weird is that?

Small Wonders

Things going bump in the night have prompted a ghost tour company to offer danger money to its guides in case they are attacked by a poltergeist.

'STRONG SPIRIT TAKES ITS TOLL', *SCOTSMAN*, 24 JULY 2000

It was the first of August. The air in the cemetery was thick and balmy, almost oppressive, a sign that a summer storm was on the way. Ben Scott had twenty people squashed in the back of the Black Mausoleum, but none of them were particularly afraid – the mood was more one of nervous joviality. David might have been plagued with sightings recently, but nothing ghostly had happened on Ben's tour in two months so he had decided that comedy was the way to go. His stories were now liberally spiced with jokes and anecdotes and, even in the Black Mausoleum, he kept up a stream of wisecracks and irreverent comments.

On either side of him stood a young boy and a girl, both about seven years old. Younger children were not common on the tours but when they did appear, Ben liked to keep them by his side. The Black Mausoleum could be terrifying enough for grown-ups – a child stuck in a dark knot of adults twice its height could get scared out of its wits. Next to the tour leader, kids tended to feel a bit more secure, and the guide could keep an eye on them in case anything happened.

Ben had decided to try to impress the crowd with his pheromone theory. It had taken him a long time to come up with it and he was damn well going to let people know about it. He stood near the tomb doorway, the lambent glow of the moon silhouetting both himself and the seven-year-olds. His full-length leather coat was polished by moonlight, the edges melding into the blackness of the tomb. He rested a leather-gloved hand on the shoulders of the children who flanked him, looking more like a demon about to unleash its minions than a man launching into a scientific explanation of the unknown. 'Ladies and gentlemen, think of this,' he began 'Ants. Ants. With legs. And feet . . .'

Ben launched into his cherished pheromones theory as if he were born to be a chemistry teacher, blissfully unaware of the crowd's eyes gradually glazing over. As he spoke, however, the two children slowly turned their heads and stared at the left-hand wall. Ben faltered and looked in the same direction, losing his concentration. He glanced down at the children, who were now staring up at him with frightened eyes. They seemed about to speak, but Ben shook his head at them and gave each of their shoulders a squeeze.

'Is everything all right?' A concerned voice drifted from the back of the vault; the children's mother. Ben looked at the crowd. Nobody appeared afraid, just worried he would start up on another chemistry lecture. 'As I was saying,' Ben continued, pulling himself together. 'Imagine it's the '70s and you are all going out clubbing . . .'

Ben Scott said goodbye to his tour at the cemetery gate. As they moved out into the street, the mother came up to him, offspring in tow. 'Thank you for paying so much attention to the children,' she said. 'I didn't realise this place would be so scary.'

Ben waved a gloved hand. 'Aw, they weren't scared.' He winked at the little boy. 'Were you?'

They boy hid behind his mother.

'Oh, they were,' she smiled nervously. 'They said they heard something laughing at the bottom of the wall.'

'Hah. That's kids. Kids are like that.' Ben, who had never considered having children, sounded supremely confident. 'And you can see how easy it is to let your imagination run away in that place.'

'I know!' The mother gasped. 'I told them that they were just imagining it.' She bent over the children and indicated Ben. 'See. The man says there's nothing in there to be afraid of. I told you there was nothing there; it's just some silly stories.'

She looked at Ben expectantly. Ben got it.

'Come here, you two.' He shepherded the children away from their mother and led them to a little patch of light under the cemetery gate lamp. He knelt down, his face now level with theirs. 'You don't have to be scared. Your mum's right. It's just some silly stories.'

He smiled disarmingly. The little girl stared at him with grim concentration.

'You didn't hear the laughing? In the wall?' she asked earnestly.

He looked into the girl's wide, waiting eyes. He turned and looked at the boy. The boy now seemed neither afraid nor unafraid. The girl stared at him, unblinking.

'Yeah,' Ben nodded. 'I heard it.'

The girl touched the sleeve of his coat, as if comforting him. 'What was it?'

He put a gloved hand on each of their shoulders once more. 'In the trade we call it . . . just-one-of-those-things.'

'What things?'

'I don't know, kid. But that was just one of them.'

The girl finally smiled and lowered her hand from Ben's arm. Ben pushed himself to his feet, pretending to lean heavily on the siblings as he did so. The children giggled. He handed them back to their mother, who thanked him again and said goodbye. Alone in the graveyard, Ben stood for a while looking up at the oily sky.

Two days later Ben Scott got a phone call from Kate.

'Guess what happened on my tour last night?' she said excitedly.

'Someone collapsed.'

'Deirdre Quirk from Ireland. She got cold and sick at the back of the vault. Said she had to get out. I said off you go. Off she went. Bang! Collapsed in the doorway.'

'Good for you.'

'It's been ages, love! Two months. I though old Mackenzie was in the huff with me.'

Ben smiled though Kate couldn't see it.

'No. He just has a strange sense of humour.'

'Eh? Oh well. Just thought I'd call. See you later.'

Kate hung up. Ben went to the window and sat for a while looking into the graveyard. The storm hadn't arrived and the sky was now azure blue.

That night Ben had a dream. In the dream he could hear his body decomposing. He could feel acid trickling down his stomach walls and his muscles relaxing like old elastic bands. He lay in his bed, unable to move. It seemed he had been unable to move for years, somehow paralysed by loneliness and fear. Mould spread up and grew under his armpits, splitting the crusty, unexercised skin and flourishing in the folds of the fat that had built in layers on his exhausted frame. Gripping hard, he squeezed oily white worms through the flesh on his arms, not sure if they were hairs or pus, or if they had eaten into him from below. He knew he was alive because he could feel his heart beating inside his chest, but as he listened the beat changed to the tick of a huge clock on the wall above him. The noise was sinister, setting his teeth on edge, and the more he tried to tune it out, the louder it seemed to get.

In the dream he opened his eyes in time to see the clock fall. The rim hit him on the flat of his forehead and the clock toppled over, its face on his face, the glass smashed, the hands pressing into his flesh. And the hands kept turning, pulling his skin further out of shape with every tick, tick, tick.

Wilson Chapel woke in the middle of the night, not quite sure what had roused him from his sound sleep. He could hear Angela breathing softly and regularly beside him. His throat was dry. He gently levered himself out of bed, put on a bathrobe and walked through the house to get a glass of water.

The kitchen was dark, though the taps glistened in the light of the moon and its image was reflected in clean plates on the draining board near the sill. Outside, the dark stonework of the graveyard wall cut across the starry sky and the silhouette of

Mackenzie's vault leered over the top like a giant bald head.

Wilson couldn't see his shed for dark shadows. Not that he used it much – he had never got over the irrational unease he felt whenever he stepped inside, as if he had somehow walked through to the tomb behind by mistake. Angela disliked that corner of the garden as well. She swore that once, while she had been sitting watching the tomb, her cup had flown off the arm of the bench without anyone touching it. Wilson felt she must have been mistaken.

He switched on the kitchen light and, as the fluorescent strip sputtered to life, the world outside shuddered out of existence. Three upturned glasses sat on the draining board in front of the now dark windows. Wilson padded over, picked one up and filled it with water from the tap, trying to peer vainly past the glowing sheen the fluorescent light had laid over the black glass. He gave up and walked back to the kitchen table, sipping his water. Looking for something to read, he settled for the back of a packet of muesli and sat down to work out what nimbo-polypropolene 4 was doing in a health cereal.

There was a sound behind him, brittle as the grinding of teeth, then a spattering tinkle, like tears falling. Wilson froze. Putting down the muesli packet he slowly turned towards the window, the place the sound had come from. Everything seemed normal. Wilson got up and walked over to the sink. Perhaps he had not turned the tap off properly and there had been a sudden spurt of water from the pipes.

'Ow! What the . . . ?' He jumped back and looked down. There were shards of glass scattered across the floor. On the draining board was the jagged bottom of one of the glasses, a grinning mouth filled with transparent teeth. It had not fallen over and smashed, because the decapitated lower half was still upright. It looked as if had been crushed where it stood.

The third glass was nowhere to be seen. Wilson searched for it, carefully moving round the splinters that littered the floor. It seemed to have vanished. He fetched a dustpan and cleaned up the mess. Eventually he switched off the kitchen light and Mackenzie's tomb sprang up over the garden wall again. Wilson got into bed carefully, so as not to wake Angela and lay trying to work out, over and over, some logical explanation for what had just happened. It was a long time before he gave up and finally drifted off to sleep. In the morning he got up early, while Angela was still asleep, and went though to the kitchen.

The missing glass was back on the draining board.

Cara

Written statement by Cara Saville about an incident which took place in Greyfriars on 8 January 2001:

My name is Cara Saville. I am 23 years old, I grew up in Warwickshire and I started working as a tour guide for City of the Dead tours in September 2000. Previously I lived in Austria and Slovakia.

In winter all the nights are very dark around here. Cloudy, icy, wet . . . it all blends into one when you are peering through the weather into a black graveyard.

Greyfriars. The name means something more to me than it does to the hordes of visitors who pass through this city looking for the statue of Bobby to photograph. The name, I realise now, is dripping with legend, myth, fantasy, call it what you like; some is fact and some is the power of imagination.

The power of imagination. Even those who have little imagination surprise themselves when they walk into that infamous cemetery late at night. I go there all the time and I've seen the calmest, coolest person, the most rock-steady atheist, turn into a shivering mass of anorak and woolly hat once we get inside the Covenanters' Prison. A recent example occurred on 8 January 2001. It was cold, had been raining heavily for two days and was very wet underfoot. My party were attempting to pick their way as delicately as they could through the mud of the graveyard. I wasn't. I like stomping along in my heavy steel toe-capped boots (the only time I ever get to wear them) and splashing grime onto the bottom of my long leather coat. A graveyard guide looks more authentic when her coat is splattered with cemetery goo.

A group of Americans struggled after me. They were having a good time but they were also having difficulty navigating the uneven terrain whilst trying to keep the mud off their impeccable, matching designer outfits. Someone at the back was trying to add to the atmosphere by making 'ghostly' noises, but that really isn't necessary in Greyfriars. The only reaction he got was from a Swiss gentleman who offered him a throat lozenge.

We reached the area known as the rogues' gallery, beside the grave of Captain John Porteous, the last stop before the Covenanters' Prison. I leapt onto one of the flat tombstones, disrespectful I know, but it looks good, and turned to face the party. The wind was picking up, causing the branches above us to creak and rustle eerily. Great. Nice and atmospheric. This area of the graveyard is always darker than the rest of Greyfriars as it is hemmed in by trees on one side and the high, ancient Flodden wall on the other – a perfect place to balance on a grave and tell stories of Edinburgh's horrible past.

I told some stories and made some jokes (people laugh very easily when they are nervous). The time had come for the warning. Did anybody know what an inductor was? People shuffled around and glanced at each other: 'Ehm . . . someone who leads an orchestra?'

I explained that an inductor was the kind of person who might attract a poltergeist, but that I wasn't worried because I already knew I wasn't one. Warning over. Right. Let's go. I shrugged off those who were clinging to my sleeves and we were on our way to the Covenanters' Prison. Chains jangled, the gates swung open and I smiled encouragingly at the white faces in my group. 'In you go.'

In they went. There was silence apart from the

squelching of feet in mud and, now that they were finally inside the prison and nobody looked like they were going to fall over unless they hit a really muddy patch, the tour party relaxed.

Before continuing to the Black Mausoleum I explained a little about the various activities that had taken place here. I told them about the Covenanters, the collapses and the cold spots.

A short blonde girl looked particularly nervous. 'It's freezing in here.' I explained that this was winter in Scotland and nothing paranormal. If she hit a cold spot she would definitely know. No matter how cold she was she would suddenly become even colder, and probably feel sick as well. All the same, the tour stamped their feet and rubbed their hands as we walked towards the Black Mausoleum. I got the rest of the questions out of the way. Was anyone claustrophobic? Anybody suffer from heart problems? Was anyone pregnant? The Swiss gentleman assured us he wasn't pregnant.

The tour party went into the tomb and I got them standing at the back. It did seem abnormally cold – far worse than it had been seconds before. I had not got far into my routine when there was a sudden shuffling at the back of the group. Someone called my name, there was a gasp of horror from the rear of the crowd and they parted. One of the Americans, a gentleman called Mike, who was wearing what had formerly been pristine white jeans, was lying unconscious in the mud.

'Is he joking? He must be messing around,' Mike's friends were whispering to each other.

But Mike wasn't messing about and his other friends were reluctant to get dirty by crouching down in the mud beside him, so I knelt to check he was all right – mud just wipes off leather trousers. He was out cold.

Mike didn't stay unconscious for long. As soon as we got him outside his eyelids fluttered, and his friends helped him to his feet. He was very white (far whiter than his jeans now were) and he was shaking. I asked his girlfriend to take him out of the Covenanters' Prison and some of his friends went too, especially when I told them they could wait for us in the pub.

Mike was all right and the rest of the tour party were anxious to talk about their experience. As has happened so often, there was far more going on in the Black Mausoleum than I realised at the time. Some of them talked about feeling pins and needles in their upper body and of the sensation being strongest just as Mike collapsed. One, Shawn Pilgren, felt 'sick and cold' just before Mike's blackout. A girl called Ariel Schudson felt 'very dizzy, weak-kneed and cold from the inside'. A man called Todd Kunkel felt 'cold in waves, with pins and needles in hands and face'.

Mike himself didn't say much, except to assure us that he hadn't been particularly scared before he collapsed and that nothing like that had happened to him before. He still looked very pale. I found out that he was an executive in some large American firm and that neither he nor his friends had ever had an interest in the paranormal. Needless to say, they had suddenly developed one and asked me all sorts of questions. I was able to answer most of them. Since I took this job I have become quite an expert myself.

This doesn't mean to say that I believe in the Mackenzie Poltergeist. Ben, Kate and David are my friends and when we sit in the pub and they talk about the things that happened before I became a guide, I admit it does astonish me. I feel the same when I see the collapses and scratches myself, though certain guides seem to experience far more than others. I have decided to blame these (alarmingly frequent) incidents on people's imaginations, even if imagination can't exactly explain the occurrences. If I allowed myself to believe there was something lurking in the Black Mausoleum I wouldn't have any fun on the tours. I'm just not as brave as the character I portray; I shut my eyes during Freddy Krueger films and I've never seen *Silence of the Lambs* or *The Exorcist*.

So why do I love to take people into the Black Mausoleum and scare them? Maybe I do believe, deep down, that there is some 'other' kind of energy at the back of that graveyard and I am experiencing something, first-hand, which other people only talk about. If that's true, no amount of fear will make me give up. Or maybe I enjoy being paid to indulge my darker side. Perhaps I long to have something happen to me, just to prove once and for all that the supernatural exists.

Then again, maybe not. I can't help thinking about something that happened to me right after Christmas 2000. I was sitting alone in my flat and suddenly noticed that my clock had completely changed its time. Now, I know there is absolutely nothing scary about that, but as I looked at the dial, which I hadn't touched, I felt an overwhelming fear combined with the absolute conviction that the Mackenzie Poltergeist had done it. It was just an insignificant little unexplained thing – nothing I could prove to be ghostly, but I was utterly convinced that it was Mackenzie's way of showing me he knew where I lived. What I felt at that moment is something I don't wish to think about, never mind write about. That's how visitors to the Covenanters' Prison feel, not me.

Let's just say I still do the job because I like to scare tourists.

Yes. That's probably it.

The Birds

Now a city ghost tour company has come under attack itself   from a Christian group which claims it is meddling with the devil . . . the Evangelical Alliance in Scotland has now written to the Church of Scotland asking them to put a stop to it because it is calling up the devil and the occult.

'Meddling with the devil is a grave mistake'
EDINBURGH EVENING NEWS, 31 OCTOBER 2001.

A spokeswoman for the Los Angeles-based Fox Family Channel, which has 79 million viewers, said, 'We have chosen the Covenanters' Prison in Greyfriars Kirkyard as one of the scariest places on earth because we are intrigued by the Mackenzie Poltergeist.' It will now feature in a 15-part series to be broadcast from March. Fox decided to devote two programmes to the kirkyard because it was thought to be the most hair-raising place they found.

'Is this the scariest place on the planet?' *EDINBURGH EVENING NEWS*, 25 JANUARY 2001

There comes a time when a joke, if repeated often enough, isn't funny any more. Or, imagine a set of scales, with one side heavier than the other. Begin to add weights to the lighter side, a tiny bit at a time. Each weight seems to make no difference. Like a plant growing, or a disease spreading, the measurement is so minute that you cannot see what is developing until you finally realise that the plant has bloomed or disease has killed it. One tiny weight, when added to many others, is all it takes to tip a scale from lightness into something much darker. It was a little brown bird, so small it weighed no more a few spoonfuls of sand, that tipped the scales for Ben Scott.

It was December 2000, the dead of winter, and a group of happy guides were gathered round a table in Greyfriars Bobby pub enjoying Christmas cheer. The interior of the bar was merry and bright, with Christmas lights twinkling under the giant sports screen.

There were now two more guides at City of the Dead tours. Kate and Ben had taken their time and picked the new members carefully; it took a certain type of person to do the job properly. The history, anyone could learn. Likewise voice projection. The real requirement to be a really good guide was an innate ability to entertain – that, and to be completely full of oneself. Despite a clash of egos that could be heard all over town, the guides got on like a house on fire and often went out drinking together; partly for the fun of it, partly to find out if anything new had happened on the tours.

And, it seemed, something always had.

On 7 August 2000, three terrified women had run from the Black Mausoleum after feeling suddenly cold and yelling to Kate that something strange was in the tomb with them. Seconds later another woman, who had been directly behind, insisted there was now something she couldn't see moving in the darkness beside her. Understandably, she also left. Five days later an American girl named Jennifer Walsh fell to the ground as Ben Scott swung open the gates of the Covenanters' Prison. Fifteen minutes later, she was still unable to stand. On 24 August an American nurse named Stacy took Ben Scott aside after the tour. Ben could tell by the way the moonlight shone on her face that she had been crying. She said that while standing in the tomb she had felt 'something beside her'. Just as she had convinced herself that this was her imagination, it laid a hand on her arm. She was too afraid to move and spent the rest of her time in the Black Mausoleum standing absolutely still, hoping not to antagonise it.

On 16 September, Leanne Callus from Edinburgh collapsed in the Black Mausoleum and had to be carried out. Four days later Elaine Holmes from Cumbernauld experienced 'something tight' against her chest, making it hard for her to breathe, and her head began to ache. As soon as she left the Black Mausoleum the sensations vanished. Less than a week after that, Radhika Hersey from California sensed 'some kind of presence' in front of her as she was about to enter the tomb and suddenly became 'freezing cold'. She decided to exit the graveyard there and then.

The eighth of October produced a student who woke up with a swollen face and eye the day after the tour. On 21 October, George Wash panicked when something clawed at his leg in the tomb. The tour party he was on also saw small floating lights above the door. Ten days later John Frank began moving around in the tomb, much to the annoyance of those pressed against him. He claimed that every time he stood still he felt a 'cold spot' move over him. Trying to work his way to the doorway of the vault, he ended up holding onto the tomb wall to keep from collapsing.

Apart from an attack on an electrician called Roy Hutchison, November was a quiet month, but in December it was business as usual. On the ninth Debbie King from London felt her legs freeze and when she reached down, the air was at a much lower temperature than the rest of the vault. She woke up the next day with scratches resembling claw marks on the backs of her hands. On 17 December Anne-Jeannette Wilson from Edinburgh felt her arm begin to go 'cold and numb' and ran from the vault. At the same time something ripped a hole in the brand-new, long leather coat worn by Paul Langton of Portsmouth. The guides were particularly worried about this new development – cuts, bruises and collapses were fine, but they now sported full-length leather coats themselves as part of the tour uniform.

Ben Scott stood at the bar trying vainly to remember what his guides had ordered. The rest sat at a large round table near the end of the room, lost in a haze of cigarette smoke and singing 'Bat Out of Hell' along with the jukebox. At one end of the table, rolling a cigarette, was Kate. Like Ben, she had remained a tour guide as well as running things. Pint of lager for her. Next to Kate sat Andrew Flowerdew, helping himself to her tobacco. Andrew was six foot two, weighed twenty-one stone and leaned threateningly towards people when he talked. With his broken nose and mop of blonde hair, he looked like he might have been an ex-heavyweight boxer, but when he spoke, his voice was gentle and humour gleamed in his eyes. During the day he held a variety of odd jobs, including gardener, antiques dealer and alcohol counsellor. Bottle of Beck's for him. Next to Andrew sat David Pollock, deep in conversation with Duncan Laird. Tall and thin with sad brown eyes, Duncan wasn't a tour guide himself, but did just about everything else in the company. Pint of lager for both of them. On the other side of the table was Cara Saville, the last member of the company. She was tall and slim with a stunning face, a cascade of auburn hair and a mind full of questions. Cara came from Warwickshire but had studied in Austria and Slovakia, and was now an odd mixture of English rose and Eastern European elegance. She was drinking something Ben couldn't pronounce, but which came in a white bottle.

Ben was the oldest of the group. Short and broad shouldered, with cropped brown hair, he was still dressed in black despite the festive occasion, acting on the theory that it was harder to look bad in dark colours. David joined him at the bar and together they loaded the table with a fresh round of drinks.

The conversation between the guides was wide ranging. Andrew was telling Kate about an American naval military exercise during the Second World War that had gone wrong and sank several British submarines. Kate was trying to decide whether to believe him. David and Duncan were discussing the hilarity of a TV advertisement featuring a drop-kicking bear. Since Duncan had graduated in film and David was an amateur moviemaker, they felt they could appreciate this on all levels, especially after a few pints of lager. Cara was playing with her hair and staring out of the window.

But, no matter where the conversation started, whenever the City of the Dead tour guides got together, it eventually turned to the events in the graveyard next door. It was Ben who started it this time.

'I saw the strangest thing in the cemetery on Saturday.'

'That was probably Kate.'

'Seriously. I saw something really weird. A really weird bird.'

'That would be Cara, then.'

'I went into the graveyard, right. This was during the day. It was lovely. I was going up the Black Mausoleum to see if it was locked.'

'Yeah. Someone keeps leaving it open.' Kate managed to glare at everyone round the table at the same time.

'Isn't me.'

'Me neither!'

'I always close it.'

'Me too.'

'No you don't.'

'Well, I usually close it.'

'Well, how come it's always open?'

'Anyway, as I was saying, I was walking up the Covenanters' Prison and this bird flew down and landed in the doorway of the Black Mausoleum.'

'So, birds are leaving the gate open?'

'Yes, that'll be it. Now can I finish my story?'

The guides nodded. Despite their joviality, they were always intrigued by any new tale about the Covenanters' Prison.

'It was just sitting there, looking inside. Like it could see something. So I walked up to it. Of course, I expected it to fly away, but it didn't. I got right up to it. Like . . . a couple of feet away. Nothing. Didn't move. I looked into the tomb, but there was nothing there. The bird was still staring inside.' Ben lit a cigarette. He was moving into full storytelling mode. 'So I knelt down beside it, right next to it, and I reached out and just . . . touched it! It sort of hopped to the side, but it wouldn't stop staring into the tomb. I poked it again and it just moved a little bit to the side, as if I was annoying it.'

'Was it wild?'

'Well, it didn't look too pleased!'

The mass groan was heard at the other end of the bar.

'No, really,' Ben spread his hands in a gesture of puzzlement. 'It was like it was transfixed – as if something in the tomb had hypnotised it.'

'What did you do?'

'Well, I suddenly realised I was kneeling in the entrance to the Black Mausoleum with a bird which seemed to be frozen by something inside that I wasn't able to see. I decided that maybe I should get the hell out. Just in case.'

'Maybe the bird was hurt or something. Was it very young?'

'I didn't ask. Thing was, when I was locking the Covenanters' Prison gate, I looked back up to where it had been sitting. It was still there but suddenly it flew off, away from the doorway, like something had startled it, or moved towards it.'

'I bet you didn't close the tomb's gate either.' Kate rolled another cigarette.

'You're damn right I didn't!' Ben looked peeved. 'But it got me thinking; you never see any birds in the Covenanters' Prison.'

'That's 'cause it's pitch black when we take the tours in.'

'You never see them during the day either.'

'I saw one,' David interrupted. 'A couple of weeks ago. But it was dead.'

'So did I.' Andrew leaned over the table. 'Halfway up the Covenanters' Prison. A while ago. Lying dead on the ground.'

'A good place for dead things to lie.'

'There's probably a cat in there.'

'You never see *any* animals in there.'

The tour guides mulled over this for a second, but not much longer. After all, it was the Christmas staff night out. It was a night for celebration.

'I tell you what,' David took a sip of his pint, 'and this is going to sound weird.'

'Anything you say usually does.'

David ignored the comment.

'When I was driving over to do the tour last week, I suddenly felt there was someone in the back seat of my car. It sounds stupid, I know, but I looked in my rear-view mirror, I was so sure. And I thought I saw something there – like a shadow.'

'Maybe you *did* see a shadow.'

'Yeah.' But he shook his head. 'I don't know. It was odd. I was sure there was something. Not a shadow. I don't know what I saw.'

'I guess it's my round.' Duncan stood up, looming over the rest of the party. 'Maybe you should just have a coke, David.'

The moment was broken. For a second the scales tipped back. Gradually the conversation turned back to the trivia of everyday life.

The next night Cara, at the head of her tour party, found a small brown bird at the entrance to the Black Mausoleum. It was dead.

The gate to the tomb was wide open.

Karyn

Statement by Karyn Perrin from Melbourne, who encountered
the Mackenzie Poltergeist on 25 March 2001:

I'm from Melbourne and have been in the UK since
October. I am working permanently in London as a
personal assistant for a top executive. I try to get away
at weekends to see different places. In March 2001 I
had four days' holiday and decided to go to Edinburgh.
I stumbled across the tour accidentally.

We had been standing in the vault for a few minutes
when I went to move a stray hair away from my face.
I did the same thing again five seconds later when,
once more, I felt something brushing my forehead. I
thought 'hang on a minute', then 'don't be silly, it's just
my hair'. Straight after, however, I felt a strange warmth
shoot right through my body. I thought this was odd,
because the guide had warned us against cold spots, not
hot spots! Before I could say anything, I suddenly felt
very strange and knew I was going to pass out. I
nudged my friend to get out of the way so I could get
outside, but he thought I was joking as we had been
laughing and having fun all through the tour, so he
ignored me. I pushed the girl in front of me out of the
way and started staggering towards the door. The tour
guide caught me just before I collapsed and helped me
outside. I instantly felt better. I didn't even have to sit
down, the feeling just disappeared.

The tour was at its end so we headed straight for
the pub where I eventually stopped shaking and my
knees stopped wobbling. The next morning I woke up

and felt my back stinging. I discovered two long scratches down the middle of my back, which were raised like a welt. They were burning and stinging like crazy. I had my friend take a photograph of them.

Later that day we climbed up Arthur's Seat [a green hilly area in central Edinburgh] and I suddenly realised that although the stinging had gone from my back, the same sensation was now on my shin. When my friend looked at my back the scratches had disappeared, but I had a large patch like a burn on my leg. It is still there, but fading gradually.

Winter of Discontent

I was wearing a thick overcoat that, until then, had kept out the cold. But suddenly there was a chill on my neck. I looked behind me into the darkness but saw nothing except my breath crystallising from my nose and mouth. I stepped two yards onto the path, but my now laboured breathing was no longer visible. We immediately decided we had taken enough photographs and walked quickly to the gate.

No one looked behind them as the padlock was snapped back into place.

'Scotland's scariest place' *DAILY RECORD*, 24 FEBRUARY 2001

February the second 2001 was the first anniversary of the death of the Reverend Colin Grant. On that day, his son, Colin Grant Junior – also a spiritualist minister – went into Greyfriars cemetery to perform another exorcism. He did so despite the misgivings of his family, who remembered the ominous statement uttered by Grant senior after he had performed the last one. But Colin Grant junior felt it was his duty to finish what his father had started.

Colin admitted he sensed a 'strong spiritual presence' in the graveyard and that the feeling changed when he reached the gates of the Covenanters' Prison. Though he disliked using the word 'evil', Grant felt that what was inside the prison was 'darker' and 'more powerful' than the presences he had encountered when instigating other spiritual matters. In fact, he had tried to go in once before only to turn back when the prison was opened. He said he had sensed a violent energy that began about six feet beyond the gates. On the anniversary of his father's death, however, Colin proceeded, going through the same ritual as his father in an attempt to lay whatever was in there to rest.

If more sprits were freed, it seemed to make no difference to the Mackenzie Poltergeist. On 9 February a visitor from Holland suddenly found he could not breathe in the Black Mausoleum. He took a few steps towards the exit and collapsed. Waking up as soon as he was taken outside, he got shakily to his feet and angrily shook off those helping him. Swaying slightly and trying to maintain what dignity he could, he strode unsteadily out of the Covenanters' Prison. His girlfriend told Ben Scott that the gentleman's name was Anders van der Lei. He was, she added, a man who was always perfectly in control of himself – she had never seen him act this way in her life. She smiled at Ben before she ran after him, and appeared rather pleased by the whole thing. On 4 March, Sophie Waters from Sheffield began to lose consciousness in the Black Mausoleum. She claimed that she felt something round her head that prevented her breathing properly. She was helped out of the Black Mausoleum just in time to prevent her collapsing completely. As soon as she set foot outside the tomb she recovered. On 25 March, exactly the same thing happened to Karyn Perrin from Melbourne. Three days later, Amanda Colley woke up the morning after a tour with bruises all over her body. A week later it was the turn of Monique Jarre from France, then Adrianne Watson from the south of England.

David stood at the gate of the Black Mausoleum with a tour party of around 25, most of whom seemed to be Australian. It was late March and the wind was dancing through the bare, winter-ravaged trees, whipping the near invisible branches into a frenzy; the tour party could hear them hissing overhead like a nest of angry snakes waiting to strike.

David delivered the company disclaimer and, after checking that nobody was pregnant, claustrophobic or suffering from a heart condition, he asked if anyone present had experienced poltergeist activity before. The crowd looked at each other and shook their heads. Then a female voice piped up from the back of the group: 'Actually, I had an experience with a poltergeist when I was a kid.'

'Okaaaaaay.' David stepped back as he ushered the rest of the tour through the gates. 'If you'd rather not go in.'

'No! I *do* want to go in. I guess I thought I'd better just warn you.' The woman elbowed herself into the middle of the crowd – she was brave, but not stupid. 'I am kinda nervous, though,' she added, rather unnecessarily.

As the group moved past into the tomb, David took the woman by the arm. She was trembling. 'If you're nervous, stay by me,' he said sympathetically. 'What's your name?'

'Alice.' She looked up at him and smiled wanly.

Though winter was reluctantly giving way to spring, the tomb was still as dark as a bad thought and the faces of the crowd were white blobs splattered on the musty background of the Black Mausoleum. On impulse, David put his arm around the woman by his side and kept it there as he talked. Suddenly, Alice's head jerked back and her knees buckled. David held her up. She looked at him and bit her lip. David glanced behind him. There was no one there. 'You OK?' he asked.

She did not reply, but gestured for him to continue.

David was proud of his storytelling ability and wasn't about to let an unexpected happening interrupt a good story. He began again, but no more than 30 seconds into his spiel, Alice jerked forward again. This time David felt her body vibrate, just below his arm. Something had punched her in the back.

He stopped the tour and walked the terrified woman outside. Taking her by the shoulders he could feel her body shaking even more than the furious branches above.

'What's going on?' he demanded.

'Something was hitting me in the back,' Alice's breath came in sharp gasps and milky puffs floated between them. 'I know it wasn't you, because I could feel your arm. It only stopped when we came outside.' She took a deep breath and managed to compose herself. 'I'm, uh, just going to wait out here until we're finished. If you don't mind.'

David most certainly didn't mind. Leaving the woman in the dark, windy passage of the Covenanters' Prison, he re-entered the tomb. The other visitors were still wedged at the back of the

Black Mausoleum, their eyes bulging so wide the tomb seemed filled with owls.

The stories that night were much shorter than normal and nobody seemed to mind, yet after David said goodbye to the rest of the tour party he was approached by two Australians and a New Zealander. 'Could you take us back in the tomb, mate?' One of them clapped David on the shoulder excitedly. 'We wanna see what it's like with just a few of us. What about it? Huh?'

David considered it. 'Not on your life.'

'Oh, come on, mate. Aren't you intrigued? Don't you wanna know what might happen?'

David looked from one to the other. 'I don't have to worry about that,' he said with finality, 'I'm back in the bloody place tomorrow night.'

'Aw, go on.'

'No.'

'Look, we'll buy you a beer afterwards.'

David stroked his chin. 'All right then.'

The Antipodeans grinned at each other. There was a cough from behind them. Alice was standing unnoticed in the darkness, half-hidden behind a large gravestone. 'I'm going back in too.'

David opened his mouth. Then he shut it again. Finally, he shrugged: 'It's your life,' he said, somewhat tactlessly.

The small party hurried back through the Covenanters' Prison and, after a bit of hesitation, entered the Black Mausoleum once more. The men walked around in the dark, feeling the walls and taking photographs.

'I don't know what you expect to see,' David said as he ran a hand over the rough stone, 'it's just a vault.'

There was a strangled sound in the corner and the men whirled round. Alice staggered backwards and hit the side of the tomb. Her eyes bulged and she gasped for breath, as if she couldn't get enough air into her lungs. David and the others gathered round her in a panic, but she did not even seem to see them.

'Get her out of here!' David grabbed the woman's arm and, with the help of the other men, he bundled her out of the Black Mausoleum. It was as if an electric current had been turned off. Alice's eyes snapped back into focus and she quickly struggled upright, all signs of her breathing difficulties gone. Apart from being absolutely terrified, she seemed perfectly fine.

'What happened?' she whispered. 'How did I get out here?'

'You had a wee problem,' David said. He turned to the rest of the astonished group. 'So. Anyone want another go?'

Nobody did.

David led them out of the Covenanters' Prison and locked the gate. He turned back and looked through the bars. It was so dark that he could not even see the offending tomb. 'Jesus,' he said quietly, 'I hope it never gets any stronger than that.'

However, Jeremy – one of the Australians – was so impressed he returned on the tour six times before his Scottish stay was over.

The guides sat in Greyfriars Bobby. It was April and there were no tours that night, for the wind was howling and rain was bouncing off the pavements. It was a melancholy night, coming near the end of a long, harsh winter and, though it was now spring, there seemed nothing fresh or new about the world. This air was reflected in the lack of conversation around the guides' table, despite the number of empty glasses. Of the City of the Dead guides, only Kate, Ben, Cara and David remained. Andrew's father had been injured in a car crash and he had left to concentrate on his counselling work, deciding to care for people rather than scare them. The remaining City of the Dead guides were dressed identically in black leather, as they always did now. It had begun as a joke and turned into just-the-way-things-were, as happens so often in life. Even Cara's golden hair was dyed jet-black.

There was little laughter in the bar and most of the seats were empty. Each guide was lost in his or her own thoughts. They were glad there was no tour. It was cold, and it had been cold for months. Somehow, too, though it was just a thought lingering at the corners of their minds, they felt that the Mackenzie Poltergeist was beginning to overshadow them and the hard work they did.

David sighed and got to his feet. He looked at Ben Scott. 'To hell with this,' he announced, breaking the mood. 'Whisky, buddy? Kate? Cara?'

'Aye. Why not?'

Seven whiskies later they were discussing the meaning of life in loud voices.

'I believe that, when you die, your soul travels to the town where you spent your first holiday.' David was expounding alternative theologies. 'It lives forever in the window of your favourite shop.'

'Damn,' said Ben. 'The Stirling Co-op doesn't have any windows.'

'You're headed for eternal damnation anyway,' Kate grinned.

'Theology,' Ben waved a drunken hand. 'Don't get me started.' Then he started. 'I'll tell you what. Take your original gods, right? Pagan, Egyptian, Greek . . . Imagine they're us, right? Sitting up on Olympus playing lutes and stuff.'

'Are we wearing those bedsheet things?' Cara always liked to know details.

'If I'm a god, I'm wearing Gucci.'

'You've got your Zeus, Hera, Aphrodite, Diana . . . Vulcan.'

'Like Mr Spock?'

'And Doctor Zeus.'

'And Doctor Spock.'

'Actually,' Kate said solemnly, 'Vulcan was a Roman god. So was Diana.'

Ben didn't even question how she knew.

'Exactly,' he said. 'All interchangeable. Be Roman if you like.'

'I'll need a new outfit then.'

'Whatever.' Ben took a deep drag on his cigarette and ash drifted down over Mount Olympus. 'The more we mortals learn, the less our gods fit with what we discover. We change our conception of the almighty to fit our growing knowledge until he becomes some blind cosmic force. An amorphous blob.'

'I have put on a bit of weight,' Cara said patting her stomach.

'In this day and age we need proof,' Ben continued, 'proof that there's life after death – that there's a point to the mess this world has always been in. Proof that there is a god who will make it all worth while.'

'No, we don't.' David sat back with his whisky. 'Lots of people just believe.'

Ben had forgotten that David's parents were religious. 'Aye,' he agreed, 'but it's getting harder, and for some of us it's impossible.' He gestured at the wall of the pub. Unseen, on the other side of the building, the graveyard and its myriad tombs glistened like the back of a giant sleeping dragon. 'What do you think that poltergeist is? I'll tell you what it is. If it really exists, it's *physical* proof that there is something beyond this otherwise pointless world. Good or bad, people want to believe in it because . . . well . . . because it means there's something to believe in.'

'But you *don't* believe in the poltergeist.' Kate put a hand on his arm.

'It hasn't done enough to convince me.' Ben took another gulp of his drink, spilling it slightly.

Kate frowned. Ben rarely got drunk, no matter how much he consumed. If he did, it was a sure sign that he was unhappy.

'I want something big to happen. One big thing out there that I can't disprove.'

'What? You want a burning bush on your tour?'

'I don't get anything happening on my tours any more.' Ben stubbed out his cigarette violently. 'I always used to. Bloody poltergeist's deserted me.'

'What about the things going on in your house?' Cara asked.

'Great. Now I don't have to go out in the cold to hear a few banging noises.'

Kate grinned: 'You never usually do.'

But Ben would not be diverted.

'It's the way we are,' he said. 'We think we adapt as the centuries go past, but that's not true. If you believe we do, try walking through the Grassmarket on a Saturday night. We've just slapped a thin veneer of bendable morals and breakable rules over our lives and called it civilisation. Deep down we're still primitive, competitive, violent, selfish and quite willing to believe in things there's no evidence for – including our poltergeist. Well, that's not good enough for me.'

'Science can explain the poltergeist.' David was playing the devil's advocate, but had got closer to the truth than he knew. 'You've been trying to prove that since we started.'

'Oh, c'mon love,' Kate pointed to Ben, 'his theories make the Flat Earth Society sound sensible.'

'I stand by science, yes,' Ben countered. 'And no, I don't rule out anything. Science is getting more and more complex and that makes more things possible to accept. Scientists have found matter so small it can't even be said to really exist, yet they say the universe is made up of this matter.' It occurred to Ben that the 'they' he was referring to sounded almost as elusive as the poltergeist.

'That doesn't make sense.' Cara was examining her whisky to see how much matter was left in the glass.

'Exactly.' Finishing his drink to avoid similar contemplation, Ben continued: 'If it's true, though, the universe isn't physical either; it's one giant thought. If that's true, there's no reason why I can't have a poltergeist at the end of my graveyard.'

'Or fairies at the bottom of your garden.'

'The point is, the more we know, the more it blurs,' Ben slurred. 'The more we know about knowing, the more we're not sure what knowing is.'

'Could you repeat that?'

'Yeah. Can you say it and drink a pint at the same time?'

'We shouldn't need religion or pseudoscience or . . .' Ben looked lost.

'Friends?'

Ben took another gulp. 'We shouldn't need astrology or counsellors or psychiatrists – not that I can afford one.'

'That's obvious.'

'Well, I give up.' Ben finished his pint with a flourish. 'I'm not responsible for the stupidity in this world. Poltergeist? I'm not saying it's true or not true anymore. I'm not playing its game. I'm not chasing it round trying to get it to prove it's really there. I'm not even going to think about it.'

'However, there is a possibility that he will write a country and western song about it.' Cara patted him on the shoulder.

'There is a possibility that I will sing a country and western song about it, yes.'

Ben smiled, for the first time that night. 'Another drink, anyone?'

Lighting a cigarette, Kate peered at him from under a fringe of hair. A small curl of smoke drifted round her head like a halo. 'You really want this poltergeist to exist, don't you?' she said.

Ben rose to his feet. Suddenly he seemed sober again, back to his old self.

'Of course I do. I'm just like anyone else, aren't I?'

The leather-clad guides looked at each other. Cara winked at Ben. David rose. It suddenly struck Kate that David looked like the photographs she had seen of Ben when he was that age.

'I'll help you get the drinks,' David said, and he and Ben went together to the bar. While they stood waiting to be served, David felt a tap on his shoulder. An elderly gentleman stood behind them. 'I hope you don't mind my interrupting.' His accent was pleasantly northern, perhaps from Skye. 'I heard you talking about Greyfriars.'

'That's right,' David said curtly. 'Pint of lager please, Ben.'

'My name's Alex,' the man said. David shook the proffered hand. 'I was at a lecture over at the museum.' He indicated the round building across the street from the bar, a towering extension added to the old Museum of Scotland which totally obscured the ancient building it was supposed to complement. In the daytime the pink edifice looked like it was built from blocks of processed ham, at night it was lit to make sure nobody missed the onslaught of progress. 'Since I was in the area I went and looked at the cemetery. The last time I was in there was a couple of years ago.'

David nodded politely.

'The Covenanters' Prison is locked now. It wasn't then.'

Ben's ears pricked up and he turned to look at Alex for the first time. He seemed like any stolid Scot, white-haired, with a whisky in his hand.

'I went in there last time, and the strangest thing happened.'

'What was that?' Both David and Ben had his full attention now.

Alex sipped his drink. He seemed a little embarrassed. 'I was walking between the tombs and I looked into one and all of a sudden . . .' Alex paused. He seemed lost in his recollection, or searching for a way to express it properly.

'Yes?' Ben and David spoke together.

'Well, I started to cry. I was weeping, actually. I don't know why.' He looked from one guide to the other with clear blue eyes. They made a strange trio, David and Ben in black and Alex in his neat tweed jacket, each almost a generation apart.

'I don't cry,' the old man said simply. 'I don't know what came over me. I mean, I don't cry.' He sipped his drink again. 'I'm Scottish.'

To Alex, this was explanation enough to make his actions astonishing.

'Was it on the left-hand side, this tomb?'

'Yes. About halfway down. How did you know?'

David and Ben looked at each other. 'You want a whisky, Alex?' Ben said.

'Och no. I just nipped in for one on the way home.' Alex shook his head. He seemed more surprised at telling this story to two complete strangers than the original incident. He finished his drink, nodded to the guides and left the bar.

David turned to Ben. 'It's a strange world, isn't it?'

'It is,' Ben agreed. 'And even stranger around here.'

Ben looked out of the window. Old Alex was walking slowly up the rainy street in the direction of the graveyard, the statue of Greyfriars Bobby staring sightlessly after him. A group of youngsters pushed past him, shouting to each other, but Alex ignored them. Perhaps the old man was of the same type as Bobby's legendary master, a taciturn, solitary Scotsman needing no more than a little dog for companionship as he marked out his time on earth. Or perhaps he had once wanted to change the world. Either way he was now just a little old man, who sat alone in bars and could not explain how he felt.

David peered round Ben's shoulder, but Alex had disappeared, like a ghost, into the night.

'What are you staring at?'

'Don't know. The future?'

David regarded the black glass, which was spattered with gusting rain.

'Really? Looks pretty dark.'

'Doesn't it just.'

And they picked up their drinks and carried them back to the table.

Raymond, Kevin, Mandy, Carol

These accounts were collected from different members of a tour party who entered the Covenanters' Prison on 9 April 2001. They called City of the Dead later to explain what had happened on and after the tour.

RAYMOND GRIEVE IS A PSYCHIC WHO HAD COME ON THE TOUR TO SEE WHAT HE COULD SENSE:

I have always had psychic ability and can sense or see spirits. Before we even got to the Covenanters' Prison, I 'saw' something: as Cara, the guide, was telling us about John Porteous, I saw a man standing next to the tour that nobody else was aware of. As soon as I went through the Covenanters' Prison gates I felt that there was an awful lot of supernatural activity. I saw a small boy inside one of the tombs near the entrance. There was also a woman farther down the Covenanters' Prison. When we got into the tomb [the Black Mausoleum] I saw a man standing outside the tomb opposite. There was another man at the bottom of the Covenanters' Prison, but we did not go down that far.

KEVIN IS 11 YEARS OLD:

When I was standing in the tomb [the Black Mausoleum], something soft, like cotton-wool, was touching my eyes and cheek. There was nobody doing this to me. The next day I woke up with a black eye and scratches on my face and my neck.

MANDY BURGEN, 25, FROM CORNWALL:

In the tomb I felt a pain just above my chest. Once the

tour was finished and I got back to my car, I unfastened my top and found a large red mark where the pain had been. I showed it to the others in the car and in front of their eyes three weals rose up in the same place. The next day they were completely gone.

CAROL WEIR, 38, FROM EDINBURGH:

As soon as the tour was finished, a number of people told me that, inside the tomb, they had felt a strange sensation all over their bodies — it was like itching or pins and needles. I was intrigued and checked my arms and face to see if I had any of the unexplained scratches the tour guide had told me about, but there was nothing. It was late when I got home so I went straight to bed. It was then that I noticed the two scratches on my right arm that had just appeared.

The Black Mausoleum

Was the exorcism a success? A week later the tours
resumed. The spirits remained defiant.
THE WORLD'S SCARIEST PLACES, FOX FAMILY CHANNEL, 19 MARCH 2001

How do you sleep at night?
(on hearing the story of the Mackenzie Poltergeist)
OUT OF DOORS, RADIO SCOTLAND, 21 APRIL 2001

Ben Scott sat alone in his room. It was Easter Sunday. Ben liked
Easter – it was guaranteed there would be a religious epic on
afternoon television, and he liked religious epics. The music was
stirring, there were lots of big stars hamming it up in little roles
and he loved the looks of awe and heroic determination on the
characters' faces. They were expressions Ben Scott felt he didn't
see much in real life.

He had led an interesting life, had done pretty much
whatever jobs came along, from toilet cleaner to financial
consultant. He'd directed a children's theatre in New York,
worked in a pornography store in Texas and painted murals in
Colorado. He'd been a cocktail barman, pepper salesman, stamp
designer and balloon decorator. He'd even worked as an Easter
bunny, looking more threatening than festive, stuffed into a large
pink fluffy costume.

Now the day had faded and he was sitting in his room. A
half-empty bottle of wine sat beside him, his only company, and
a cigarette coughed dirty smoke from the ash-filled pool of an
old eggcup.

Once Ben had felt indestructible. He had cultivated an
enigmatic persona and charmed women with this careless,
carefree disguise. His delight had been the late night smoky bar,

drink in one hand, cigarette in the other and a story on his lips. Now he felt old before his time, and tired. His back hurt – he had jumped from a train into a snowdrift in the Rocky Mountains and the injury had never healed. Ben's stomach hurt too, the result of years of hard drinking combined with the ever-present feeling that his life had been nothing more than a series of exotic memories. Now they were fading like a photograph in a sunlit window.

Ben Scott was afraid. Afraid of being alone. Afraid that nothing meant anything. Afraid to sleep. Afraid of disappointment. Afraid of death. And he realised that, somewhere along the line, he had become afraid of life. He wondered if this was because he loved life too much. Perhaps he couldn't bring himself to care about something that would be taken away from him. Perhaps because of this he had never really become involved in life at all. Ben knew he was merely watching his existence wandering past, and had done so for as long as he could remember. He sat in a musty tomb created by his own fear, and watched an endless stream of strangers pass in and out. Sometimes he tried to reach out and touch them – and when he did he succeeded – but then he would retreat back into the darkness before anyone could really see him.

Ben was at a loose end this Easter night. He had rearranged all the photographs in his photograph album, as he liked to do – he could look at the pictures and remember a little of how it had felt to be in them. Then he threw away any in which he wasn't nice looking, in case he died of a heart attack before he got round to ditching them. Now there was nothing left to do but drink and smoke and think about how much he was drinking and smoking. At a push, he supposed, he could think of life and what it all meant, but that was an activity he tried to avoid unless it was daylight. He knew the other guides were in Greyfriars Bobby Bar and that he could go and join them, but jovial banter was too much of an effort these days. Ben had done a lot of talking over the years. He didn't think he had much left to say. All his life, he had gone where fate had taken him, and now it wasn't taking him anywhere. Or perhaps he had spent his life running from commitment, from responsibility, from any door that might close. Perhaps nobody expected anything from him any more and so he had nothing left to run from.

Ben Scott was feeling pretty sorry for himself.

There was a loud swish of bead curtains from just outside the living-room and the bathroom door suddenly closed. Ben got up and went into the hall. He put his hand out and held it at various heights, but could not feel a draught. He returned to the living-room. The half-empty bottle of wine sat on his desk, the cigarette silently burning itself out next to it. Beside his own glass sat an empty one meant for a friend who, in the end, he couldn't be bothered inviting.

The living-room door had swung open as he stood looking at the four walls in which he now spent his life. He turned and regarded the bead curtains, splendid in their fluorescent green, now as quiet as an expectant pause. 'Are you real?' he said in the direction of the motionless sparkling beads. 'You're more real than me, I think. People believe in you.' He looked at the clock on his wall. It was nearly midnight.

Fetching the ladder from the hall, he dragged it into the living-room, pulled up the blind on his window, opened it and pushed the ladder out until it sank into the soft earth of the graveyard below. He put on his long, black leather coat and stuck his cigarettes in the pocket, opened his cupboard, took out a flashlight and put that in his pocket too. Then, taking his bottle of wine and the empty glass in one hand, Ben levered himself out of the window and climbed down the ladder into Greyfriars.

It was as black a night as he had ever seen in the cemetery. There were few stars, and no sign of any moon. The church was nothing but a shapeless lump of coal and the tombstones were oily black stumps. The trees were bare and twisted. Greyfriars looked like hell with the fires put out.

Ben began to walk towards the Covenanters' Prison.

There was a soft wind blowing and it whispered as it danced along the grass. Ben took the middle path, which skirted the church and headed up towards the locked gates. His flashlight illuminated a tiny patch of ground in front of him, which only made the rest of the graveyard seem darker. Despite his best efforts he could not help shining the torch at each tomb he passed in case someone, or something, was hiding there. The beam lit up skeletons and skulls and sad testimonies from those long dead. As he rounded the church he finally glimpsed the moon, a small sliver of light like a half-shut eye, hanging over the Covenanters' wall, not bright enough to even dent the shadows. Ben reached the gates, brought out his keys and opened the near-invisible padlock with an ease borne of long practice. He stepped inside and began to walk down the dark alley of the Covenanters' Prison. On impulse he stopped and walked back the way he came, then took out his keys once more and locked the gate behind him.

It seemed colder in here, but that might be because the chill spring air was finally getting to him. Puffs of wispy condensation escaped his lips as he made his way towards the Black Mausoleum. On either side the doorways of tombs, slick with recent rain, gaped hungrily. Or perhaps, Ben thought, they were open-mouthed at his stupidity. With the gates locked he knew he was completely alone. If anything was going to confront him here, it was not going to be human.

He reached the Black Mausoleum and stood looking at it. It seemed no different from any other tomb. Across from its entrance was a low wall. Ben sat down on it and poured himself a glass of wine. 'Well,' he said, 'here I am.' He lit a cigarette. 'So what do we do now? Sing "Kumbaya"?'

The Black Mausoleum stayed silent.

'Thirty-eight seems a bit old to finally acquire an imaginary friend.' Ben looked around. His eyes were getting used to the darkness. The branches of the trees overhead were deathly still and he could hear no wind, nothing but the quiet sound of life that was his own breathing. 'You know, I used to live in America,' he said to the Mackenzie Poltergeist. 'I went to a cocaine factory. I've been chased by a bear.'

The mausoleum seemed unimpressed.

'I've never seen the Grand Canyon, though. Never been to Las Vegas. Have you?'

Ben looked around again. The sliver of moon was reflected in puddles and wispy touches of silver gilded the grotesque carvings that surrounded him. It suddenly occurred to him that the Covenanters' Prison right now was as beautiful as anything he had ever seen. 'I bet there are people who come here that have seen the Grand Canyon and are just as impressed with you – in a different way, of course.' Ben sipped his wine, then raised his glass to the mausoleum gate. 'Hell, I can bring you people from Las Vegas. Everyone takes a gamble when they come to see the Mackenzie Poltergeist.'

The tomb stayed silent.

'I suppose I should just come inside, eh?' He stood up and put down his glass, walked over to the door, then stopped. 'But I always find that when you get right inside something, or someone, you've nowhere left to go.' He put his hand in his pocket and pulled out his bunch of keys. Finding the one that unlocked the Black Mausoleum padlock, he bent down to open it.

The vault padlock was gone.

Kate had done the tour earlier that night. Kate *never* left the gate unlocked.

Ben felt a jolt in his chest. He shone the flashlight in a wild arc. The padlock lay broken a few feet away, glistening in the damp grass. The hairs on the back of Ben Scott's neck slowly began to rise. Aware that he had his back to the tomb, he whirled round and shone the light inside. There was nothing but cold, empty stone. 'Don't you do this to me,' he said softly. But it was too late.

Suddenly Ben Scott felt afraid. He was not numb; he was not tired; he was afraid like he had never been afraid before. A second ago he had been ready to enter the tomb, sing a few bars of a folk song and walk back out again. Now his skin was crawling, his teeth were set on edge and a primitive grimace was locked onto his face. He couldn't go into the tomb. He knew it with a certainty he had rarely felt. Terror, deep and thick and cold as the bottom of the ocean, prevented it. He did not know if he was terrified that he would find the poltergeist in there or if he was terrified he would not. All he knew was that he didn't want to know.

He turned and ran full speed back up the Covenanters' Prison, leaving his wine and cigarettes behind. His keys scrabbled at the lock on the gate and he flung it open and slammed it behind him again. He ran through the graveyard between crosses and skeletons and tombs and, as he ran, he began to jump, landing heavily on the pliant earth and kicking up wedges of soil. He stopped halfway and did a little dance, his heart pounding in his chest. Then he ran again and didn't stop until he neared the graveyard exit. His breath came in ragged gasps and he bent over, holding his knees. 'Jesus. I've got to stop smoking,' he told himself.

The exit of the graveyard was like a gateway to another dimension. The cemetery lamp, set in an iron arch over the exit, signalled the end of one place and the beginning of somewhere very different. Through the narrow rectangle Ben could see the lights of the Museum of Scotland and, as he got closer, a car flashed past along the street outside, like a giant shining bug. Deserted tenements rose in cliffs on either side and, as he moved into their shadow, they blotted out the stars one by one.

Ben stopped before turning into the exit. There wasn't a sound in the graveyard. Outside he could hear the crude buzz of night revellers punctuated by drunken yowls. Like ants, they crawled from one bar to another, fighting, mating, and swarming. In here the ground was filled with humanity who no longer served a purpose, outside they walked around, only a breath away from their silent cousins. They didn't even know it.

Ben Scott bent and touched the soft, wet grass. 'I spend too much time in this damned place.' Then he walked out of the cemetery.

From the graveyard entrance to Ben's front door it was just 20 yards, the only thing between them being the big bow-fronted windows of Greyfriars Bobby's bar. Some of the individual panes had swirling glass ampoules, giving the place a

Victorian look. Ben peered inside. He could see Kate, Cara, David and Duncan talking, laughing, smoking and drinking, as people had done in there for 200 years. The light from the windows spilled onto the pavement, showing up the litter.

Ben stood on the wet pavement. The cold Easter wind blew out of the graveyard entrance like a last breath being exhaled. He took out the keys to his front door. In his house the fire was on and he could drink wine and smoke cigarettes and not have to bother speaking, or listening, or caring. In his house he could sit on his window seat and stare out into the darkness of the cemetery.

Ben looked round at the statue of Greyfriars Bobby. Someone had put a traffic cone on the dog's head. For a second he pursed his lips, the way old people do when nothing amuses them any more. Then he began to laugh. The door of the pub opened. A group of teenagers, jostling and giggling, poured out of the brightly illuminated bar into Candlemaker Row.

Ben Scott put his keys back in his pocket and walked past them into the light.

Kate

Written statement sent by Kate Luskin from Massachusetts in May 2001. Kate entered the Black Mausoleum a month earlier on 15 April 2001, the night before Easter Sunday.

My name is Kate Luskin and I was on a trip to England and Scotland a few weeks ago. I went on a City of the Dead tour and I was scared out of my wits by what I felt when we entered the Covenanters' Prison, and especially the Black Mausoleum. I was right at the back of the tomb and began to feel really dizzy and faint.

The tour guide, Cara, told us that if we suddenly got cold, or felt something was touching us, we should immediately move from the spot where we were standing. Then I felt something ice-cold hooking on to my ankle. I quickly moved away – I thought I must just be overreacting and I didn't want to tell anyone what had happened. But I started to shiver and couldn't stop. It was all too much and I began crying.

After the tour was over I was still shaking and shivering, but I was sure I had just scared myself. Yet my left ankle was cold and stayed that way for the rest of the night and the next day. I play softball, and am developing a tan from being out in the sun so much. Now there are three lines on my left ankle where it was touched in the tomb and they will not tan – they stay pale no matter how much I am in the sun. This has never happened to me before. There is nothing odd on my left ankle, only on my right – the marks look like nail scratches but are not red and simply will not get darker. The odd thing is, that part of my ankle is now always freezing cold.

It probably sounds stupid, but it's starting to freak me out a little.

Epilogue

Kate, Ben, David and Cara still lead City of the Dead tours into the Covenanters' Prison. Derek has even returned to do an occasional tour, his dream job turning out to be not quite so great in reality.

The Mackenzie Poltergeist is stronger than ever and its attacks seem to have increased in scope and severity. It is now regarded as one of the most conclusive and best-documented paranormal cases in history.

Despite the poltergeist's fame, or more likely because of it, visitors still take the tour, stand in the darkness and hope that something will happen to them. After all, they don't *really* believe they will encounter a supernatural entity on a ghost tour in the middle of the capital city of one of the most civilised countries on the planet.

Until they do.

Bibliography

Campbell, Thorbjorn, *Standing Witnesses* (Saltire Society, 1994).

Dick, William, *From Castle To Abbey* (Scottish Automatic Printing, 1947).

Doren, Charles Van, *A History of Knowledge* (Ballantine Books, 1991).

Fraser, Joy, *Never Give Up the Ghost: A Folklorist Analysis of the Ghost Tour Industry* (MA Thesis, Department of Folklore, Memorial University of Newfoundland.) [Copy housed in the School of Scottish Studies, University of Edinburgh. For details email e99jf@mun.ca]

Grant, James, *Cassell's Old and New Edinburgh* (Cassell, 1880–83).

Keay, John and Julia (ed.), *The Collins Encyclopedia of Scotland* (Harper Collins, 1994).

McGonagall, William, *Collected Poems* (Birlinn Ltd, 1992).

Pirsig, Robert M., *Zen and the Art of Motorcycle Maintenance* (Morrow, 1974).

Smellie, Thomas, *Men Of the Covenant* (Andrew Melrose, 1903).

Stevenson, Robert Louis, *Picturesque Old Edinburgh* (Albyn Press, 1983).

Stone, Reuben, *Encyclopaedia of the Unexplained* (Amazon Publishing, 1993).